CORE POWERED
GOLF

The Revolutionary FitBall® Training

Program to Increase Distance,

Consistency and Accuracy

Neil Wolkodoff

K·P
KickPoint
Press
Denver, Colorado

CONTENTS

Core Training Exercises 49

Overview of the most effective exercises for golf and their correct execution, both in strength/power and flexibility maintenance and development.

Core Routines 93

Key training areas of the golf stance, rotational energy, rotational power and in-season counter-balancing programs are presented with additional routines for warm-up and flexibility development.

Training Equipment 121

How to select, care for and inflate the FitBall® for your needs and additional equipment which can help take your core training further.

Glossary 125

Index 129

ABOUT THE AUTHOR...

Neil Wolkodoff, Ph.D., sport scientist, trains both professional and amateur golfers in physical training and mental training for golf. He has trained a variety of athletes including NFL, NHL, MLB and Olympic athletes for over 15 years. A former strength and conditioning consultant for the Denver Broncos, the Colorado Rangers and the U.S. Freestyle Ski Team, Wolkodoff now devotes his efforts to helping golfers improve their performance. He holds certifications from the American Council on Exercise, the American College of Sports Medicine, the U.S. Weightlifting Federation and the National Strength and Conditioning Association.

He is a past contributing editor for the American Council on Exercise, past editor for the American College of Sports Medicine, as well as contributor to various golf publications such as *Golf Digest*, *Golf Magazine* and *Golf Tips*. Wolkodoff is a sport science consultant for GolfTEC in Denver. His nationally recognized clinics on the physical and mental aspects of golf are sanctioned for continuing education credit by the PGA and LPGA.

His numerous awards and accolades include Best Personal Trainer in Colorado, 1997, by the *Denver Post*; State Director of the Year from the National Strength and Conditioning Association (twice); "80 People in Fitness to Watch in the '90s" by *Fitness Management Magazine*; and *Self Magazine* citing Wolkodoff as "one of the best exercise physiologists in the business." His Physical Golf Training Center is located at the Greenwood Athletic Club in Englewood, Colorado. He can be reached via the internet, www.physicalgolf.com.

E

CORE POWERED GOLF

GET CORE POWERED!

Golf may be the most difficult sport in existence. Other professional athletes outside of golf as well as countless amateurs strive to have a better golf game by trying new clubs, taking more lessons and trying a myriad of swing training devices. In reality, these devices have done little to improve the overall handicap of most golfers. With the current wave of sophisticated technology in golf equipment, golf performance as measured by overall handicap and driver distance has only improved marginally if at all. Your body is the most important tool in golf.

The realization is here that golf is a sport, not just a game, and you should be in good overall athletic condition to play and improve to your best level. While specific sports conditioning was scoffed at just a few years ago for golf, it is now commonplace for serious amateurs as well as professionals to pursue year-round fitness and conditioning programs for golf.

Physical Improvement = Better Golf

As one gets older, the notion that one can continually improve performance in any sport for an indefinite period of time just by participation is quickly diminishing. Technique in golf is dependent upon the physical abilities to apply that technique. For example, forearm power as well as hip and back flexibility are key physical attributes for golf performance, yet are not developed or maintained just from playing golf. The older golfer has possibly even more to gain from improving golf fitness and specific abilities. Simply put, combining enhanced physical abilities, course management and wisdom enables the older golf athlete to be a better golfer than when they were younger.

For the older athlete, maintaining core power and flexibility is not likely to occur from daily activities or just playing golf. Physical conditioning programs, blended with other factors contributing to a healthy lifestyle, can retard the aging process and, in some cases, can return the body to physical performance levels reached 20 to 30 years earlier. The old adage "if you don't use it, you'll lose it" definitely applies to fitness and golf.

Junior golf athletes also have discovered that physical training can give them an edge over the competition and improve their golf just as much as new clubs or more lessons. Because physical training is gaining in importance from the amateur to the professional level, an early introduction to physical training is physically and mentally beneficial to the junior golfer.

Core Training Directions

Physical training has purposely mutated over the last 10 years to include better training methods for specific parts of the body and specific sport movements. Training the trunk or core has been recognized to be key to improving sports performance. Over the last few years, there has been an explosion of training techniques and devices designed to improve everything from abdominal appearance to increased sports power.

The use of a FitBall®, (inflatable sport training balls ranging in size from 22 to 30 inches in diameter), has been gaining in popularity as a method to improve stomach and back muscles and gain flexibility. In golf performance, these muscle groups have multiple functions for the swing, yet may be the least trained by most golfers. The FitBall® training program outlined in this book will quickly, easily and effectively develop a range of abilities from Core Power to flexibility. The results will be longer drives, a more consistent swing and decreased back and general injury potential.

Golf Specifics

Golf involves the lateral storage, rotation and then release of energy through the club down the target line. Without the key muscular abilities of the core muscles, this sequential movement won't be very powerful or consistent. The body must maintain the optimal position of the spine being essentially "stacked" over the pelvis or hips, or the chance of an efficient and powerful swing sequence is greatly diminished.

Another significant performance factor not often thought of by golf athletes is dynamic balance. During this lateral and rotational storage and release of energy, there is almost a figure-eight weight shift from the target toe to non-target heel, up to the non-target toe, then back to the target heel. While subtle, this weight shift helps to re-direct this energy towards the target line. Training on a FitBall® has the added benefits of developing dynamic balance and awareness of body position, both of which contribute significantly to the golf swing.

Core Training Focus

Many golf injuries are caused by the inability of the golfer to maintain proper spine angle in the swing, thus putting more stress on other muscular groups besides the back. The knees, hips, forearms and shoulders often are subject to extra stress to compensate for a lack of core abilities. In addition, golf is a sport where rotation along the spinal axis is extremely important, possibly more so than in any other sport. Yet most training programs rarely address these rotational dimensions and muscle groups.

If you are already a good golfer, can the core training program outlined in this book help your golf game? The answer is definitely yes, both from a performance and longevity perspective. Get a more conditioned core, and you will play more consistent and powerful golf. Gain core power and flexibility, and you will hit the ball farther and gain accuracy no matter what your level of golf.

A good physical training program, one geared to your fitness level and the requirements of golf itself, will increase performance for a golfer at any level of mastery. While the focus of this program is core conditioning and training, you also need to pursue training for the other fitness components of overall body strength and power, flexibility and aerobic or cardiovascular conditioning.

So what can the core or trunk conditioning program outlined in this book do for your golf? Here is a summary of the ways the exercise programs in this book will improve your golf performance and quality of life.

Power off the Tee. The name of the game in golf is club-head speed, and core training improves your ability to generate club-head speed through a better spine angle which results in more mechanical power from a more effective swing sequence.

Decreased Back Injuries. When you exercise your trunk regularly, you counteract the stress and tension of daily life, as well as the physical demands of the golf swing. Golf can be tough on the back, and it is definitely more debilitating if your swing is different every time because of the lack of muscular endurance or flexibility.

Finding Your Swing. As you improve your core muscles, you can effectively use the other physical components and muscle groups to develop your most effective swing. Without the proper function of your back and trunk, you might never reach your full potential, no matter how many lessons you take or how many new drivers you try.

Better Posture. If your muscles get in balance, front to back and right to left, your overall posture will improve. Core muscles of the trunk provide support not only during the golf swing, but also in daily activities such as walking, driving and sitting.

Less Body Strain. Because the golf swing requires the body to function in a sequence, the lack of trunk strength and rotational ability in some golfers means more stress to the shoulders, arms and legs. Training the core lets these muscle groups function at their optimum in the golf swing chain, both in power potential and flexibility, improving overall mechanics and decreasing injury potential.

Time-Sensitive Training. Using a FitBall® has the added benefit of working a number of fitness factors from flexibility to power into one exercise. Almost all exercises in this program work on more than one muscle group, and add the dimensions of dynamic balance and body awareness. The result is that you will train effectively and have more time for golf.

Core training for golf is relatively simple, yet requires consistent application. The programs in this book and the partner video of "FitBall®-Power Golf" are aimed at first building core stability, then adding the ability to rotate along the axis of your spine in the swing, and then developing the ability to maintain this alignment, rotate and then add rotational power. In addition, you will find in-season programs to counter-balance the negative effects of regular golf and improve your flexibility.

Remember, golf is a sport. As a golf athlete you are dependent on the abilities of your trunk or core to help you perform more effectively and powerfully. This program will improve your golf game.

References

Adams, Mike, and Tomasi, T.J. 1998. *Break 100 Now.* New York: Harper Collins Publishers.

Baltes, P. B., and M. M. Baltes. 1980. *Plasticity and Variability in Psychological Aging: Methodological and Theoretical Issues in Determining the Effects of Aging on the Central Nervous System.* Berlin: Shering.

Bortz, W. M. 1996. *Dare to be 100.* New York: Fireside.

Chopra, D. 1991. *Perfect Health.* New York: Harmony Books.

Delmonteque, B., and S. Hays. 1993. *Lifelong Fitness.* New York: Warner Books.

Evans, W., I. H. Rosenberg, and J. Thompson. 1992. *Biomarkers: The 10 Keys to Prolonging Vitality.* New York: Fireside.

Hosea, T.M & Gatt, C.J. 1996, Back Pain in Golf. *Clinics in Sports Medicine,* 15(1).

Wilmore, J. H. 1986. *Sensible Fitness.* Champaign, Ill.: Human Kinetics Publishers.

Wolkodoff, N. E. 2000. "Stabilize Your Swing." Golf Magazine. p. 160. April, 2000.

Wolkodoff, N.E. 2000. "How to Survive Your Golf Vacation." *Golf Digest Magazine,* pp. 139-142. March, 2000.

UNDERSTANDING THE GOLF SWING

The Perfect Swing = Core Control

Golfers live for the perfect swing and the resulting perfect shot. Unfortunately, this is not a common but an uncommon occurrence for most golfers. Just about every golfer wants more distance and wants it consistently. While there are many muscle groups involved in this complicated swing movement, your core or trunk muscles are the key in allowing the lower and upper body to work together effectively. In addition, the core muscles also produce their own amount of core power and rotational energy.

Physical Dimensions of Golf

The golf swing is a highly complicated activity that takes coordination from both sides of your body for both movement and maintaining body position. You need balance, flexibility, specific psychological skills, power, coordination, endurance, and strength. These are needed in the right quantities in the proper muscle groups for the optimum golf swing.

Because the average PGA touring pro has a swing time ranging from approximately .95 to 1.25 seconds (which includes the start of backswing to impact), golfers need tremendous muscular control to initiate and consistently make the right swing for the right situation. The speed of the swing means that so much muscular activity occurs in about a second, it's difficult to feel which muscles are activating, let alone activating most efficiently in the proper sequence. Awareness of your trunk and core muscles is almost impossible at this speed of movement, yet control is essential for a repeatable and powerful swing. Like other fitness factors, if your total time swinging in a round plus practice is on average three minutes, you can't expect to gain or maintain core control and power just by hitting golf balls.

It is often obvious that flexibility and strength is important for a part of the golf swing. *Knowing what to do with a body part or muscle group during the golf swing does not mean you have the physical ability to do it*. To act in a coordinated, consistent and powerful motion in golf, the muscles have to have the right blend of power, strength, endurance and flexibility. The physical capabilities of the muscular system, especially the trunk and body core, will in a large part determine your golf swing.

The Power Link

Like a chain, the golf swing is dependent upon all the needed muscle groups making a contribution. The golf swing is a function of your physical ability to have all the mechanical elements contribute in the right timing and repeatable execution of the swing. Optimal conditioning of your trunk links the lower and upper body and allows the muscle groups to harmoniously work and produce a powerful and consistent swing.

Strength and power in one muscle group are dependent upon another muscle group to make the application for golf. Even if muscle groups such as the shoulders, legs, forearms, or back possess the right physical qualities and yet your trunk can't rotate, store and apply the energy in the swing, the swing will be less than 100% effective and will be random rather than repeatable. An effective golf swing is one where the arms, legs, trunk and shoulders coil or store energy, and then release and direct that energy so that maximum consistent impact occurs with the golf ball. Power is a function of the rotational energy potential produced by the kinetic or stored energy in the backswing, a function of the turn versus resistance, coined the "x" factor. The arms and shoulders utilize this plus some additional energy on the path through the downswing, which is tied to another source of energy, the weight shift towards the target, which moves the axis or rotational point of the swing towards the target. The core muscles are important to all three of these energy sources with contributions ranging from stability to rotational energy.

Any weak link in the chain causes force to be lost somewhere in the golf swing. From this perspective, golf is a total-body athletic event; almost every major muscle in the body contributes to the golf swing and should be enhanced using physical training. The core or trunk of the body links these various muscle groups.

The path to a better golf swing is really quite simple—your physical abilities will directly affect your respective swing characteristics. Increase the abilities, and you have the physical foundation to improve the golf swing whether your goal is distance, consistency or accuracy.

In the case of core muscular abilities, without the flexibility needed in your hips and low back, there may be a tendency for tempo or timing issues. For example, without the specific ability to rotate your hips towards the target, you are likely to over-use your arms and use them earlier than if you possessed flexibility in this area. An effective golf swing needs to have a weight shift to the target side, then the flexibility in the hips to begin to rotate, and then finally have the arms and shoulders continue the whip-like action and catch up at impact. Without the key core functionality, the swing sequence won't be optimal. These same core characteristics of flexibility and power also significantly add torque or twisting movement during the downswing and through impact.

Personal Swing Power

Discovering and understanding your own physical limitations and strengths of your core is of paramount importance when attempting to find a swing that's right for you. If you can't make the movement, it simply may be that your body is not physically capable of making the movement.

The fitness conditioning effect from just playing golf is minimal at best. Strong back, abdominal and hip muscles are important to golf, yet aren't developed effectively from repeated golf swings during a round. In an average round, where the golfer shoots 100, only three minutes of total time is spent swinging the club, including practice time.

Sports Fitness, Golf Fitness

Every sport requires some degree of strength, power, endurance, and flexibility. Golf is no different in that it requires specific physical abilities which include:

- Strength, which is defined as the maximal force you can exert regardless of duration.
- Power, or the ability to perform a movement as rapidly as possible.
- Muscular endurance, the ability to repeat a movement, including the basic golf posture or address position, without fatigue.
- General endurance or aerobic capacity, which is the ability of the whole body to work steadily over an extended period of time.

• Flexibility, which is your range of motion around a joint or set of joints.

Golf is a sport that requires muscle endurance because the swing is repeated, especially on the practice range in short succession between shots. Power is necessary for each shot because in most cases, a golfer is best off generating as much controlled club head speed as possible. Strength is important to maintain body position and posture, such as the spine angle during the swing. The core musculature must possess all these abilities for a golfer to be at his or her maximum potential during an entire round of golf.

A major difference between the pro tour players and amateurs is golf-specific flexibility. The tour players get a greater degree of shoulder turn from trunk rotation than most amateur players, who gain this turn mostly from the shoulders and lose valuable kinetic or stored energy. Without the spine and trunk twisting along its own axis and the back knee serving as an axis point, you're forced to use other muscles to generate both the swing and club head speed. The results are often a less than repeatable swing, erratic distance with the same club, high injury potential and fatigue. Training the core muscles for golf may be more important for the amateur golfer than the tour professional for this reason.

Swing Basics

During the golf swing, a number of complex movements occur which are inter-linked in flexibility, muscular endurance, strength and power. During the basic stance, in a flexed position, you rely on support from your hamstrings, or the back of the upper leg. Without adequate strength or flexibility, the hamstrings will tighten, causing the right or non-target knee to straighten during the backswing. In addition, strong muscles in the back and abdominals are essential for support and maintaining support during the golf swing. Balance, posture and swing mechanics are, in this case, direct results of physical capabilities, especially in the trunk region.

In golf you use both sides of your body, and both sides are active during the swing. During the take-away or backswing in a one-piece take-away, your shoulders turn away from the ball while your arms initially stay fully extended, with a relaxed grip on the club. In some players, there is an active hinging of the wrist and elbows, which requires more muscular activation of the arms, shoulders and forearms.

Your weight then shifts from being evenly distributed between the feet to the back foot, or non-target foot, while the hips turn away from the ball. The hips turn as a result of the shoulders turning, not as an independent movement. In this "coiled" position, you then un-coil the hips with a slight-to-moderate hip motion towards the target while coordinating with the arms and shoulders to meet the ball with as much speed and force during impact as possible. The swing continues with a weight shift to the target foot and a follow through with the club, arms and shoulders.

Phases of the Modern Golf Swing

For the purpose of core training for better golf, the golf swing phases will be matched with the major trunk muscle groups primarily responsible for movement and golf posture. Because the golf swing is a movement with individual variations, swings may look similar, yet they are not 100% identical. The human body is a lever system for golf, rotating around the shoulder closest to the target. The side closest to the target is referred to as the "target side," whereas the opposite side of the body, in the case of a right-handed golfer, the right side, will be referred to as the "non-target side."

Some research indicates that the muscle groups used are essentially the same for amateurs as professionals, just the efficiency and consistency varies based upon proficiency. For example, tour pros fire the muscles in short bursts only when they are needed. High-handicapped amateurs may fire or activate the muscle throughout the entire golf swing. It may be, that as an amateur, your need for conditioning from this perspective is substantially higher than tour players. For example, the tibialis anterior or front of the shin, a muscle used in balance, is often repeatedly fired by amateurs with high handicaps to maintain balance. On the other hand, the swing mechanics of tour professionals are so consistent that they rarely get out of balance, so this muscle group is much less activated than with amateurs.

Address/Basic Stance

In this position, the golfer has weight equally distributed with approximately 60% on the non-target side and 40% on the target side. Most golfers can fit the hips in between the width of the ankles during address. The knees are slightly bent (10 to 20 degrees) with the back bent slightly forward, partially as a result of the hips tilting forward five to 15 degrees. The fingers and hands grip the club in this position with a straight or close to straight arm, with the back of the palm or the target hand facing the target. The target shoulder is slightly higher than the other shoulder. Some muscles of the upper body adjust and stabilize to maintain the distance from the golf ball.

Core/Trunk Muscles Used/Action

Trunk - Erector spinae (back): posture/balance during eccentric, or lowering contraction.

Rectus abdominis (abdominals): posture/balance.

Training Implications

Starting with the golf stance or address position, the trunk muscles are important determinants of golf posture. If you don't possess strength and muscular endurance in the golf stance and basic address, you won't maintain consistent posture through your round. As you change your golf posture over 18 holes, your mechanics have to change. Unfortunately, this usually

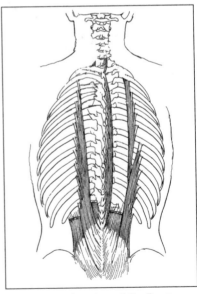

Back or anterior view of the Erector Spinae group, a primary stance muscle group and spinal rotator.

means less than optimal results. Without adequate trunk strength starting in the stance, other muscle groups are going to have to compensate during the swing sequence.

BackSwing

During the backswing, a number of muscle groups become active which were not active in the stance. In the backswing, most golfers start to take the club and arms back as a unit, with the club being perpendicular to the plane of the shoulder.

Your hips and shoulders begin to rotate (with motion started by the shoulders) away from the target, with the shoulders ultimately 35 or more degrees of rotation away from the target than the hips. This difference between the shoulder and hip turn is referred to as the "X factor." During the backswing, the weight shifts from a fairly equal distribution to weight approximately 85% on the rear or non-target foot because of the redistribution of upper body mass.

As the arms and shoulders try to move backwards as a unit, more muscle groups are called into play, and those which were active become more active.

The external obliques (side abdominals) on the target side as well as the hamstring contribute to initiating hip rotation and controlling hip rotation during the backswing. The entire upper body moves slightly away from the target towards the non-target foot. Both the target arm/side and follow through side/arm contribute to the take-away.

Core/Trunk Muscles Used/Action

Trunk - External oblique (side abdominals), target side: rotation along spinal axis.

Internal oblique (side abdominals), non-target side:

rotation along spinal axis.

Rectus abdominis, non-target side: rotation/stabilization.

Erector spinae, non-target side: back stabilization, rotation along spinal axis.

Quadratus lumborum: trunk stabilization.

Core Training Implications

Without adequate flexibility in the spine and hips, the golf athlete can't get to the most powerful backswing position, one where the shoulders have turns almost twice as much as the hips. This position also takes muscular control for the trunk to not over-rotate or get outside of your base of support in such common faults and over-rotation.

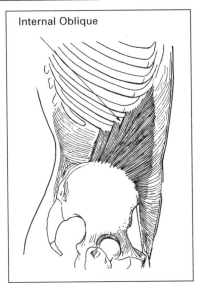

Internal Oblique

The Internal oblique, side angle, an active spinal stabilizer and rotator.

The Downswing/Initiation Forward

During the downswing, the weight distribution moves to the target side both from the un-coil/turning of the hips into the target, and the shift of the entire body towards the target as a rotating, lateral and pivoting movement. Before the downswing, the shoulders are turned approximately 35 degrees more than the hips. The stored energy in the muscles, ligaments and tendons plus the stretch reflex (see Chapter 4 on flexibility), as well as your brain saying "now swing," all contribute to the movement.

Better golfers move their hips as the initial movement of the downswing, while others move the

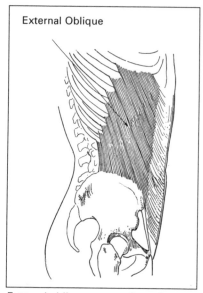

External Oblique

External oblique as seen from the side, a primary muscle of trunk rotation.

hips/shoulders simultaneously. Like throwing sports, the movement of the hips in golf initiates the motion. The non-target arm and elbow angle should be less than 90 degrees, which facilitates the generation of angular velocity.

Core/Trunk Muscles Used/Action

Trunk - External obliques, non-target side: stabilizers, pulling of shoulders towards hips and rotation towards target.

Internal obliques, target side: trunk rotation.

Erector Spinae, target side: trunk rotation.

Quadratus Lumborum: Lateral trunk flexion.

Golf Training Implications

To make the weight shift needed to initiate the downswing and start rotating the hips takes significant trunk control and flexibility. The trunk must maintain spine angle while rotating and directing energy.

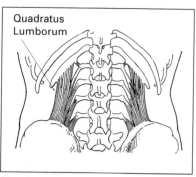

Quadratus Lumborum

The Quadratus lumborum, a spinal stabilizer and spinal bender, as seen from the posterior or back view.

Impact

During impact, the target arm and non-target arm and club should be extended as a singular unit to maximum length. The non-target side, especially in the trunk area, has activated the abdominal region to help launch the movement of the body, forward and laterally to the target. At ball impact, certain muscle groups, such as the target side internal obliques are extremely active. At this point in the golf swing, the mechanics and muscle groups activated in the initiation and acceleration of the downswing either remain active or decrease activity.

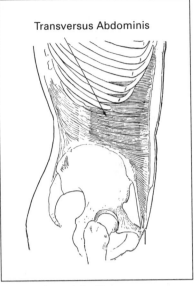

Transversus Abdominis

Lateral view of the Transversus abdominis, which stabilizes the spinal column.

Timing of the various lever systems at impact is critical to club head speed and control. The hips and shoulders decrease the angular distance between them in terms of amount of turn, due in part to the rotational speed of the shoulders being faster than the hips, as the hips have reached full rotational velocity somewhat before, and now that rotational energy is carried farther by the extension of the shoulders and arms. Full extension of the hands/forearms at impact is required for maximum club head speed. This lateral-then-rotating movement towards the target is another determinant of developing club head speed.

Primary Muscle Used/Actions

Trunk - External obliques, non-target side: pulling of shoulders to hips and rotation towards target.

Internal obliques, target side: trunk rotation.

Rectus abdominis: stabilization.

Erector spinae, non-target side: trunk rotation.

Quadratus lumborum: side bend of trunk on non-target side.

Golf Training Implications

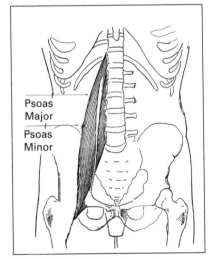

Psoas Major

Psoas Minor

The Psoas major and minor, seen from the anterior or frontal view.

The combination rotation /lateral movement towards the target of the entire body is based upon hip and leg rotation. Exercises for the adductors, abductors and other hip muscles are essential to adding hip power. The hamstrings aid in maintaining posture and help rotate the femur and

hips towards the target. The hamstring group and abdominals are very active during this phase of the swing.

Follow Through

During this phase of the golf swing, most muscle groups don't have as much activity; the swing with a few exceptions is a continuation of momentum, weight change and the extension of energy down the target line. Even though momentum carries a large part of the follow through, it is dependent upon certain muscle groups to continue the movement toward the target while maintaining balance. In addition, some muscle groups such as the rectus abdominis contract or perform a "braking" function to keep the golfer from hyper-extending the back.

In this phase of the golf swing, the golfer's center of gravity has shifted totally to the target leg. In addition, the shoulders and hips have rotated towards the target so they are facing the target, with the non-target side shoulder slightly closer to the target than the target side.

Primary Muscles Used/Action

Trunk - External obliques, non-target side: stabilizers, pulling of shoulders towards hips and rotation towards target.

Internal obliques, target side: trunk rotation

Rectus abdominis: stabilization and isometric contraction at end of swing to prevent excessive hyper-extension of the back.

Erector spinae, both sides: brings upper body/trunk upright at end of swing.

Training Implications

The abdominals are still active, both in the end of rotation and in stabilization. Strong

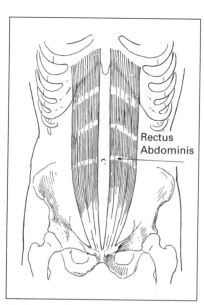

Rectus Abdominis

The Rectus abdominus, frontal or anterior view, which the lower portion acts as a spinal stabilizer.

trunk muscles, not just the abdominals, are important for golf, as they are active in every phase of the golf swing.

Observations Which Dictate Core Training

The Golf Swing as Whole-Body Movement

The golf swing uses upper, trunk and lower body muscles. Muscle groups which might not contribute to the active swing play just as important a role in posture or maintaining consistent swing planes. To a large degree, the right and left sides of the body function as mirror images of each other, even though your force and movement is directed towards the target. The target side, the left side if you are a right-handed golfer, is not necessarily more important than the other side of the body.

One of the training principles that can be derived from this analysis is that core training should involve the basic movements of trunk flexion (forward bending), extension (rearward extension), lateral flexion (side bending), rotation (twisting along the long axis), and stabilization.

During powerful swings and stances with less than optimal footing and support, you may call other trunk muscles into use which are important stabilizers and movers. The transversus abdominis, which runs laterally from just below the rib cage to the pelvic area in the front of the body, contributes to overall trunk stability. The psoas major and minor form the back of the abdominal wall and run longitudinally from the lower spine to the hip and upper leg. Like the transversus abdominis, the psoas group appears to respond to the need to balance the spine, much like ropes supporting a pole, especially when the person is out of balance in the spinal area. This muscle group also will aid in laterally flexing the spine. Training on a FitBall® will result in strengthening these key stabilizers, which are called into action during off-balance and out-of-normal tempo swings.

Spanning The Ability Globe

Golf is a unique sport in that in one motion your muscles have to perform with abilities ranging from muscular endurance to power. Your physical training should reflect the specific abilities these muscle groups need. In the core musculature, you need all the possible movement patterns reflected from endurance to power, with the flexibility needed for your optimum mechanics.

Injury Potential

Golf results in many injuries that just shouldn't occur when considering the nature of the sport–a highly coordinated, whole-body movement where the muscular stress is spread through almost the entire body. The sheer magnitude

of the force generated in a single golf swing dictates that the weak links will be more susceptible to injury. The average golf ball weighs 45+ grams, yet it is stationary at impact while your body is accelerating as fast as possible. The back, elbows, wrists, shoulders and knees are susceptible to injury if they are the weak links in this powerful and dynamic motion.

And that is the point: golf is powerful yet unnatural at the same time. Without specific conditioning for all the core muscle groups, you won't have a consistent, efficient and more powerful swing. Treat golf as a sport, and train your core musculature away from golf to improve your swing, lower your score and reduce your risk of injury.

Summary

- Golf requires the use of almost all the muscles in the body for an effective golf swing, and the core musculature is the link between the upper and lower body.

- The golf swing for most people is not a natural motion, therefore physical training can enhance the abilities to make the swing effective and repeatable.

- The golf swing simultaneously uses core abilities for strength, power, muscular endurance, and flexibility.

- Almost every major core or trunk muscle in the body is used in the golf swing.

- The target side and non-target side core muscles are both essential to a sound and repeatable golf swing.

- The unique requirements of golf mean that core or trunk training not only improves performance but reduces injury potential.

References

Cochran, A., and J. Stobbs. 1966. *The Search for the Perfect Golf Swing.* New York: J.B. Lippincott Co.

Jorgensen, Theodore, P. 1999. *The Physics of Golf,* second edition. New York: Springer-Verlag Publishing.

Kawashima, K. 1993. Comparative analysis of the body motion in golf swing. International Society of Biomechanics. Congress (14th : 1993 : Paris, France); Societe internationale de biomecanique. Congres. (14e : 1993 : Paris, France). In, *Abstracts of the International Society of Biomechanics, XIVth Congress, Paris, 4-8 July, 1993,* vol. I, Paris, s.n., 1993, 670-671.

Kirby, R., and J.A. Roberts. 1985. *Introductory Biomechanics.* Ithaca, NY: Movement Publications Inc.

Knudson, G., L. Rubenstein., and N. Harris. 1989. *The Natural Golf Swing.* Bellevue, WA: Kirsh & Baum Publishers.

Lowe, B., and I.H. Fairweather. 1994. Centrifugal force and the planar golf swing. World Scientific Congress of Golf (2nd: 1994: St. Andrews, Scotland). In, Cochran, A.J. and Farrally,

F.R. (eds.), *Science and Golf II: Proceedings of the 1994 World Scientific Congress of Golf, London*, E & FN Spon, 59-64.

McLaughlin, P.A., and R.J. Best. 1994. Three-dimensional kinematic analysis of the golf swing. World Scientific Congress of Golf (2nd: 1994: St. Andrews, Scotland). In, Cochran, A.J. and Farrally, F.R. (eds.), *Science and Golf II: Proceedings of the 1994 World Scientific Congress of Golf, London*, E & FN Spon, 91-96.

McTeigue, M., S.R. Lamb., R. Mottram., and F. Pirozzolo. 1994. Spine and hip motion analysis during the golf swing. World Scientific Congress of Golf (2nd : 1994 : St. Andrews, Scotland). In, Cochran, A.J. and Farrally, F.R. (eds.), Science and Golf II: *Proceedings of the 1994 World Scientific Congress of Golf, London*, E & FN Spon, 50-58.

Montague, L. 1993. The ABC of a perfect golf swing. *Golf News*, 4-7.

Nesbit, S.M., J.S. Cole., T.A. Hartzell., K.A. Oglesby., and A.F. Radich. 1994. Dynamic model and computer simulation of a golf swing. World Scientific Congress of Golf (2nd : 1994 : St. Andrews, Scotland). In, Cochran, A.J. and Farrally, F.R. (eds.), Science and Golf II: *Proceedings of the 1994 World Scientific Congress of Golf, London*, E & FN Spon, 71-76.

Sanders, R.H.; Owens, P.C. 1992. Hub movement during the swing of elite and novice golfers. *International Journal of Sport Biomechanics* 8(4):320-330.

Wallace, E.S., P.N. Grimshaw., and R.L. Ashford. 1994. Discrete pressure profiles of the feet and weight transfer patterns during the golf swing. World Scientific Congress of Golf (2nd: 1994: St. Andrews, Scotland). In, Cochran, A.J. and Farrally, F.R. (eds.), Science and Golf II: *Proceedings of the 1994 World Scientific Congress of Golf, London*, E & FN Spon, 26-32.

Weir, B. The Attacking Golf Swing. 1992. *Golf Australia* 31-35.

White, A.L. 1991. *Validation and Comparison of a Model Golf Swing with the Mechanical Profiles of Beginning Golfers.* Thesis (Ph.D.) Ann Arbor, Michigan: University Microfilms International.

3
CORE POWER

Strength and power are normally thought of as qualities you build in the weight room, yet the training program outlined in this book and demonstrated in the FitBall®-Power Golf video enhance your consistency and distance by building muscular endurance, strength and power in your trunk muscles. Core power and strength will result in a stronger, more powerful swing with better consistency.

"Strength" really covers a wide range of abilities, from muscular endurance to power. Depending upon the sport's requirements and on how one trains, sport-specific strength is a unique blend of physical abilities and sport performance needs. In golf, strength in your core is the ability to hold a position, then develop rotational control and power around that mechanically correct and efficient position. Core strength and power is first posture, then rotation with spinal control and finally rotational power down the target line.

Golf is a demanding sport from a strength and power perspective. Each time you swing, you store and then re-direct energy down the target line and through the golf ball with as much force and control as possible. Core power is the link between upper body and lower body power, and will make your golf both more powerful and more consistent.

Additional Performance Factors

Any sport relies on a blend of performance factors, not the least of which in the case of golf are balance and kinesthetic or space/time awareness. Using a FitBall® will also improve balance, timing and general body awareness in a single exercise because of the demands you are placing upon your body. Balancing upon the ball or just maintaining a posture/position while performing certain movements at a given speed will increase your kinesthetic sense, or the ability to feel your body in space and time, a key component to building and maintaining a solid golf swing.

The Big Picture

Your muscles will respond differently to various types of core strengthening exercise. Not only must you perform the right core exercises for golf, but at the optimal level or intensity, and with the best method for both your golf swing and level of physical training. There is no one "Core power" but a whole continuum of qualities ranging from muscular endurance to strength to power. Understanding these qualities and how they affect golf performance will help you select the right exercise variations to maximize your golf potential.

So, which core "strength" qualities are needed for golf?

Muscular Endurance

On one end of the strength spectrum is muscular endurance. This is the ability to perform submaximal, or less than all-out, effort for an extended period of time. In competitive cycling, for example, muscular endurance is important because of the large number of leg revolutions needed at 80+ rpm to complete a 25-mile race. In golf, muscular endurance is important in the erectors because of their need to support you in the basic stance for each swing.

Muscular Strength

Strength is defined scientifically as the ability to produce maximal force regardless of the duration involved in doing so. A good example is a wrestler trying to maneuver his opponent while also maintaining his position. Certain muscle groups in golf use significant strength levels. The hamstrings and obliques are two of the key core muscles that maintain certain positions during the swing. Strength is needed in order for these muscle groups to maintain golf-specific posture, balance, and control.

Power

Power is an area golfers have long recognized as critical for generating club head speed. Power is defined as the ability to move as rapidly as possible or to overcome a resistance in the shortest possible time. Golf over the last 10 years has become more power-oriented with the emphasis on added distance. In reality, power is a function of the swing sequence combined with optimal mechanics. That is why after a point, adding very heavy resistance to a FitBall® exercise, such as a 20 pound medicine ball, may result in little if any power gain since one muscle group just isn't solely responsible for power production. However, some extra power can be developed from adding speed or a light resistance, such as a heavy med ball of one or two pounds to an exercise such as the wood chop crunch. Power in golf is dependent upon sequencing, not absolute force production like football.

Eccentric or Lowering Strength

By scientific definition, eccentric movements are where the muscle lengthens, generally controlling a lowering movement. In the stance, the erectors in your back are fighting gravity when they lower to the static position of address.

Static Strength

Static strength is the ability to hold a position, and that ability with respect to spinal alignment is key for golf. When fighting a force such as holding a position, the small protein filaments of the muscle essentially lock-up for short periods of time with the effect being no or little movement.

Physiologically, static or isometric strength has a high correlation with eccentric, or lowering abilities.

Balance & Functional Strength

Functional strength is the combination of basic strength abilities plus your coordination at applying each particular quality at a specific time in a movement that attempts to simulate the actual sport or movement demands. Because the exercises in this program utilize balance, movement and stability, they can all be classified to some degree as building functional strength. Balance is your ability to control your body position counter to the forces in the sport, and FitBall® training can be a great balance developer.

Types of Muscular Contractions or Movements Used in Golf

To improve golf performance in training with the FitBall®, you need the right combination of strength factors in your training movements. These basic movement types are called muscular contractions. Not all provide the same benefit for golf performance, so you need to make sure all these types of muscular contractions are used in your core training program.

Concentric contractions occur when the muscle shortens, as when you pull a weight toward your shoulders in a bicep curl. Lowering the weight back down as the muscle lengthens is an example of an *Eccentric*, or lowering, contraction. Normally, you can lower 50% more weight or resistance than you can raise because of the physiological nature of muscle contractions.

Another type of contraction important to golf performance is the *Isometric* or static contraction, where muscle is used to push against resistance that is sufficient to prevent much, if any, movement. An example of this type of contraction is the back bridge exercise, where you are fighting gravity without movement.

Functional Training

Functional abilities which require balance, stability, posture, movement and reaction are all important in golf. By combining other exercise devices such as balance discs and heavy med or plyometric balls, you can further challenge your stability and balance. However, you should only attempt advanced functional training with extra resistance or instability devices once you have developed good core stability. Also, remember that trying to simulate the golf swing is of little value in adding to these abilities, as the golf swing is a precise firing of specific muscle groups in a sequence and can't be duplicated outside the context of the actual swing.

Factors Involved in Core Development

In addition to the way muscle reacts to core training, there are other factors that help determine your training program's effectiveness in improving your golf performance.

Progressive Overload

Without consistently increasing the intensity or volume of your training, you won't progress. Whether it is muscular endurance, strength, or power you want, it is necessary to make your training workouts progressively more difficult. At each training session you should strive to do one more set, one more repetition, add a heavy med ball, rest a little less between sets, use a slightly larger or smaller FitBall®, or add a disco sit under one foot to further challenge your balance.

Training Variety

The more ways you can perform the same resistance training exercise, the better. For example, you can alternate single side bridges with basic back bridges on successive days, or alternate between two different FitBall® sizes. Having exercise choices for a specific muscle group is important in keeping the muscle stimulated into making continual gains. Training variety also maintains strength during the golf season, when you may only pursue resistance training once a week. Variety can help you make the most of limited training time.

The Core Golf Progressions

Golf first involves stability of the spine, then rotation around that spinal axis. The exercises in this program in the Golf Stance section are designed to build core stability and your ability to hold the optimal address position. Once your core muscles are trained for these static or holding movements, then you can begin to add rotational movements; in this case these are the exercises in Rotational Energy. After you can rotate along the spinal axis with stabilization, then you are ready to add the power exercises in Rotational Power.

Because golf involves the constant overuse of certain muscle groups, the Counter-Balance routines address this need by getting your posture, strength and flexibility back into balance so you can play optimal golf for the entire season. How much you perform the various routines is a matter of time and training need.

- Golf requires core muscular endurance, strength, and power for successful performance.

- Muscular endurance is the ability to repeat a movement without fatigue, such as repeating the golf swing on the practice range.

- Strength is the ability to exert maximal force regardless of the duration involved in doing so.

- Strength for golf specifically involves eccentric or lowering movements, which aid in maintaining posture and directing force through the swing.

- Static strength, or the ability to hold a posture or movement has more relevance for the golf stance or basic address position.

- Power is the ability to exert maximal force in the shortest possible time, and therefore is a contributor to greater club head speed.

- Functional strength and agility are the ability to move through space and time in various movement patterns efficiently.

- Different core muscles used in golf have varying requirements for the best combination of muscular endurance, strength, and power.

- Golf will not build the necessary strength, power, or muscular endurance in your core required for optimal golf performance.

- Core training will enhance flexibility for golf if performed correctly and with balance in respect to opposing muscle groups.

- Overloading, or constantly presenting more challenge to the muscle, is the key to both building and maintaining strength gains.

- The Golf Stance exercises stress core stability and form the foundation for rotation and power.

- Rotational Energy routines challenge your core by adding rotational movements to spinal stability.

- The Golf Power routines combine stability, rotation and more powerful movements and more difficult positions which further prepare the core to work optimally in the golf swing.

- The Counter Balance routines are designed to be used during the golf season to reduce the effects of always swinging to one direction. These routines will place the body back into muscular balance for optimal mechanics and overall posture.

References

Burke, R. E. 1986. The Control of Muscle Force: Motor Unit Recruitment and Firing Patterns. In N.L. Jones., N. McCartney, and A.J. McComas., eds., *Human Muscle Power.* Champaign, IL: Human Kinetics.

Chu, D. 1996. *Explosive Power and Strength: Complex Training for Maximum Results.* Champaign., IL: Human Kinetics.

Costill, D. L. et al. 1979. Adaptations in skeletal muscle following strength training. *Journal of Applied Physiology* 46:96.

Dominguez, Richard H, and Gajada, Robert. 1982. *Total Body Training.* New York: Warner Books.

Hurley, B. 1994. Does strength training improve health status? *Strength and Conditioning Journal* 16:7-13.

Komi, P. V. 1979. Neuromuscular performance: Factors influencing force and speed production. *Scandinavian Journal of Sports Sciences* 1:2-15.

——.1986. The stretch-shortening cycle in human power output. In N. L. Jones, N. McCartney, and A. J. McComas, eds., *Human Muscle Power.* Champaign, IL: Human Kinetics.

Matveyev, L. 1981. *Fundamentals of Sports Training.* Moscow: Progress Publishers.

Melby, C. et al. 1993. Effect of acute resistance exercise on postexercise energy expenditure and resting metabolic rate. *Journal of Applied Physiology* 75(4):1847-1853.

Noth, J. B. 1992. Motor units. In P. V. Komi, ed., *Strength and Power in Sport*. Oxford: Blackwell Scientific Publications.

Radcliffe, J., and R. Farentinos. 1985. Plyometrics: *Explosive Power Training*. Champaign, IL: Human Kinetics.

Reichley, Melissa. "Roll with It: Swiss Ball Techniques.: Advance for Physical Therapists." September 6, 1993: 10,25.

Sale, D., and D. MacDougall. 1981. Specificity in strength training, a review for the coach and athlete. *Science Periodical on Research and Technology in Sport* (March).

Tesch, P.A., and P. Kaiser. 1984. Muscle capillary supply and fiber type characteristics in weight and power lifters. *Journal of Applied Physiology*, 56:35-38.

Wilson, G. J. 1991. Stretch shortening cycle: Nature and implications for human muscle performance. *Journal of Human Muscle Performance* 1(3):11-31.

Wolkodoff, N. 1987. Mixing rest with workouts. *American Ski Coach* 10(5):
——. 1991. Plyometrics. *IDEA Today* 9(3):32-36.

CORE FLEXIBILITY

Flexibility is key to consistency, accuracy, and power in your golf game. It aids coordination, helps with hip rotation and swing mechanics, and in certain cases reduces injuries. As with other fitness components, just playing the game is not enough to develop optimum flexibility for golf. The use of a FitBall® is an excellent means to build golf-related flexibility.

Flexibility Enhancement

Research indicates that increasing range of motion (ROM) is essential for golfers because if you lack adequate flexibility, you simply won't have tour-level mechanics. Overall flexibility is enhanced by using this program because you are not only moving through a full range of motion, but you are also building muscular balance and strength abilities.

Problems in your current swing patterns may not be the result of inadequate swing training or practice. They may stem from reduced ROM in the key joints and muscle groups of the hips and low back that don't allow you to swing to your full potential. Improving this ROM means that you will be able to explore new swing patterns and movements. Flexibility is necessary to allow the body to coil in the turn like a spring and then effectively uncoil into the downswing.

The repetitive nature of the golf swing and the muscular imbalances it can cause heighten the need for the golf athlete to pay attention to flexibility levels in the trunk. Thus, it is important for a flexibility enhancement program to maintain key abilities and counter-act the repetitive and over-use nature of the golf swing.

The Kinetic Link in Golf

As a golfer, you'll find that tight muscles are often associated with lack of strength, overuse injuries, and muscular imbalances in other areas. The hamstrings are a perfect

example–they're used constantly in the golf stance and also help to rotate the hips during the downswing. However, few golfers ever train or even consistently stretch this muscle group. Thus, it becomes a chronically inflexible area exacerbated by the repetitive demands of the golf swing. When the hamstrings loose functionality, chances are the golfer will try to compensate with other muscle groups, which then become tight and out of balance. A functional problem with one muscle group can soon become a problem with a number of muscle groups in the golf swing.

The more balanced your fitness program and the more emphasis you place on ROM activities, the less need you'll have for formal stretching. This is one of the reasons that core training on a FitBall® is one of the best overall exercise routines–it simply promotes muscular balance, therefore enhancing basic flexibility levels.

Can You Be Too Flexible for Golf?

Too much ROM can hamper rather than help your golf game, especially in the backswing or take away position. This is especially true in the relationship between the hip, back, and hamstring muscle groups. Avoid pushing your ROM too far beyond what golf requires in any of the key muscle areas. Otherwise, you will probably lose some of the force that can be activated by the "stretch reflex" at the top of the backswing.

The stretch reflex is a protective mechanism designed to keep muscles and joints from overextending. When a muscle is stretched close to its maximum range, a set of sensors called muscle spindles sends a signal to the brain that the muscle is being over-stretched. The brain then sends a signal back to the muscle that activates a reflex response, thus heading off injury from over-extension. The speed and duration of a stretch helps determine how powerful any stretch reflex activation will be. For example, at the top of the backswing, if there is a slight amount of muscular tension from a stretch in the shoulders and hips, that tension activates the stretch reflex. This stretch reflex will help the muscles to fire or activate with greater force on the downswing.

Golfers with faster swing tempos are more likely to become over-stretched and lose power in the backswing. The tendons, ligaments, and muscles store "elastic" energy released in a golf swing in a way that is similar to propelling a rubber band by stretching and then releasing it. The combination of a high swing speed, short backswing, and low total swing time is especially hurt by excessive ROM. Being overly flexible in the backswing or full take away position for this kind of golf swing means the stretch reflex doesn't activate as powerfully, thus some force production is lost from the swing.

When combined, the stretch reflex and stored elastic energy can help increase the power of a golf swing. However with too much flexibility you can't effectively use either of these power-generation mechanisms. If you have a short total swing time, then performing a combination of active, dynamic, and static flexibility training exercises will work best. This combination will allow you to use the stretch reflex effectively. If your swing is relatively slow, then you should gear more of your training toward static stretching methods, which don't activate the stretch reflex in the opposite direction. This will allow you to precisely and slowly control backswing and downswing motion.

With regard to the impact position and the follow through, extra flexibility which allows a greater follow through will generally increase distance and club head speed. In this sense, the more you can accelerate through impact and beyond, the longer you can make shots. To this end, if you have extra time, you might stretch the muscles involved in free follow-through more than those in the backswing position.

Basic Flexibility Training Methods Used in Sports

Static, or Reach-and-Hold: In this method you stretch to a specific position, then hold the stretch, normally for 10 or more seconds.

Ballistic Stretching: In this method the muscle is pushed so far with active movement that it stretches back rapidly like a tight rubber band that has been released, utilizing the physical elasticity of the muscle and the activation of the nervous system (stretch reflex). For example, the V Rotation exercise in the bridge position, if done rapidly to the extreme ends of range of motion becomes a ballistic exercise because the stretch reflex will provide part of the power for the return movement to the other side.

Active Flexibility: This type of flexibility is demonstrated in sport movements or stretches where one muscle group, when activated, forces the opposing muscle group to relax while it is pulled through a range of motion. The Advanced Trunk Rotation stretch when pushed to the limits of your r.o.m. will force the muscle groups not contracting to relax.

Passive Flexibility: In this method a training partner or external force, such as gravity, is used to push a muscle or limb beyond its normal range of motion. The Side Stretch, where your trunk is stretched through gravity pulling you around the ball, is an example of passive flexibility.

Dynamic Movement: This method relies on sets of exercises that gradually push the joints and muscles through greater range of movement over a period of time. It refers especially to the use of alternating muscle groups, as in the Squat To Arch, where you are alternately contracting then relaxing the rectus abdominus and the erector spinae to add range of motion through the prescribed number of repetitions.

The FitBall® stretches included in this program are actually various combinations of these various flexibility methods. Based upon your swing needs, you should explore various combinations of different types of stretches.

Golf: A Dynamic Game of Static Proportions

Static flexibility is related to your ability to move through a muscle's ROM regardless of speed and to hold it for at least a short period of time. Holding a split position in gymnastics is a good illustration of static flexibility. If you have a very low swing speed, static flexibility is more important at the top of the swing position. Dynamic flexibility is related to ROM during active movement, normally a fairly rapid movement. Examples are a very quick golf swing, the movements of a runner's legs during sprinting, and a basketball guard making very rapid direction changes. In each of these movements, the rapid movement in one direction is followed by a movement to the other direction.

Training for golf is really best approached by developing both forms of flexibility. There are times to use methods that promote static flexibility and other situations to use methods that promote dynamic flexibility. It all depends upon the type of golf swing you have and the ultimate purpose of the stretching exercises. With the flexibility exercises that can be done on a FitBall®, you can perform most exercises as dynamic or static, thus tailoring the exercise to your personal flexibility needs and current fitness level.

Static methods are best at relieving muscle soreness and apply best to movements that occur very slowly. For some golfers with very slow swing speeds, increasing static flexibility is important in the trunk. For golfers with moderate or faster swing speeds, dynamic or movement-based flexibility is important in the shoulders and the hips and has a bigger effect on improving golf performance with the base of enough flexibility to make the mechanically correct swing movements. In this program, if you need more movement-based flexibility, then you can dynamically perform such exercises as the advanced trunk rotation to add this physical dimension.

Active and Passive Stretching

Active stretching is applicable to golf because it builds strength balance as well as flexibility. Some of the exercises such as Squat To Arch and Advanced Trunk Rotation also develop balance and body awareness. In this method, you use the muscle group or groups that oppose the ones you want to stretch in a motion that is opposite of the action of the target muscle group. Activating one muscle group means the opposite muscle group will relax (known as "reciprocal inhibition") and can then be more effectively stretched. Because active stretching involves repeated contractions, the movement muscle group eventually gains strength from the repeated movements, further enhancing strength balance, a requirement of permanent flexibility.

Individual Flexibility Application

The key to optimal golf flexibility is to match your body type with your swing patterns, swing speed, and physical training preferences. Not everyone is built the same way, so no two golfers should stretch the same way. Your goal is to discover which blend of the exercises in this book is most important to your golf game, and you may find that just performing the strengthening exercises on the FitBall® will help develop flexibility as well.

Guidelines for Stretching

Stretching every day is preferable to a marathon session once a week, which will only increase your risk of injury and won't improve your flexibility. Like other forms of exercise, stretching should "overload" the system to force both permanent and short-term changes. In stretching, you have to push slightly beyond your limits if you expect those limits to change. Stretching exercises should stress proper mechanics and alignment.

Static stretching is excellent for relieving muscular soreness and for building static flexibility. In addition, joint systems susceptible to injury, such as the back, benefit more from static stretching because of its lower potential for causing injury. Remember that the faster your swing, the more important movement-based and active stretching, such as the Squat and Arch will be to your golf performance. Active flexibility, where one muscle group pulls as the opposing group relaxes, has a high correlation to improved facility of movement. Because of the relationship of static stretching to relieving muscular soreness, using a FitBall® right after golf or physical training will aid in reducing muscular distress.

Strength Balance, Permanent Flexibility

Remember, golf is a sport that is extremely dependent upon the trunk muscles to be in balance all the way around the core. A useful analogy is a suspension bridge, where function and structural integrity is dependent upon each cable system exerting an equal amount of force. This same analogy is also why some golf athletes have chronic flexibility problems with their hamstrings and low backs, those muscle groups are constantly overpowered by stronger quadriceps or affected by weak abdominals.

For flexibility to be permanent flexibility, it is important to get the system back in balance. In the case of the hamstrings, it means extra sets of leg curls or Pelvic Hip bridges. Keep the system in muscular balance, and you can decrease your need for formal stretching exercises. The stretching exercises in this program are meant to work in conjunction with the stabilization and strengthening exercises used in this program.

Back Specifics

Stretching the back is complex because of the multitude of ligaments and musculature that support the spine, as well as the movement limitations of each vertebra. The spine is more susceptible to injuries caused by rapid movements, which can cause damage to disks and ligaments, especially if you can't maintain the proper spine angle during the swing. Golf is tough on the back, and in most cases, gentle movement stretching and static stretching are preferred methods of increasing spine flexibility, especially when first starting a golf conditioning program. Once you have developed the ability to maintain spinal alignment and have adequate rotational ability along the spinal axis, then you can begin to add more dynamic exercises and stretches.

Get Back to Posture

Without some daily or every other day core exercise, most golfers will not have the strength or flexibility to consistently maintain the best golf posture through a round or a season. Regaining good posture should be a goal of both your strengthening and stretching programs. If posture is an issue for you, perform more bridge exercises and add some time in each of the stretching exercises, especially those which move you in the opposite direction of your normal golf stance.

Stretching After Exercise or Golf

If you go through a formal exercise training session, FitBall® or otherwise, then static stretching after your routine will improve flexibility and alleviate muscle soreness. Stretch the muscles used in your training regimen as well as those that are your weak points in golf. After a round of golf, you have moved your muscles an average of more than 200 times in the golf swing, including practice swings, and your muscles are relatively warm. You'll be less sore, especially in your overworked muscles, if you stretch after your round. Concentrate on hamstrings and the core. Two to three minutes of static stretching in the clubhouse on the FitBall® will decrease muscular soreness and allow you the added mental benefit of being able to focus on an analysis of your game or practice.

If you are new to training for golf, use more stretching exercises than you think you might need because most golf athletes over-estimate their flexibility levels. As you gain fitness and pay more attention to proper warm-ups and muscular balance, you will discover that you can cut back on the amount of additional flexibility training you perform. Like other fitness factors, flexibility is much more difficult to build than to maintain.

Summary

- Muscular balance is a requirement for permanent flexibility, so perform the complete routines in this program, not partial routines.

- Stretch daily in some form, preferably on the FitBall®, yet stretch in some form.

- Never stretch a cold muscle. During static stretching, always stretch after the exercise routine or after golf.

- When you perform movement-based stretching using either dynamic or ballistic stretches, such as the Squat To Arch, start with a limited range of motion and gradually increase the range of motion through 10 to 15 repetitions, or until you become fatigued.

- A combination of methods, including static, dynamic, and limited dynamic/ballistic stretching, should be your training goal. Using all three of these methods in your workout will produce results superior to exclusive use of traditional static stretching.

- The faster your natural tempo in both backswing and downswing, the more your flexibility program should be geared toward active and dynamic stretching, which can help your body take advantage of the stretch reflex to generate more power.

- To heighten the relaxation effect from stretching, breathe deeply and completely during the 15-20 seconds you hold each stretch, and never hold your breath during a stretch or movement.

- Gaining flexibility on the FitBall® has the additional benefit of improving overall balance and kinesthetic sense or body awareness.

References

Asmussen, E., and F. Bonde-Petersen. 1974. Storage of elastic energy in skeletal muscles in man. *Acta Physiologica Scandinavica* 91(3):386-392.

Bates, R. A. 1971. Flexibility training: The optimal time period to spend in a position of maximal stretch. *Master's thesis, University of Alberta.*

Bird, H. 1979. Joint laxity in sport. Medisport: *The Review of Sports Medicine* 1(5):30-31.

Broedelius, A. 1961. Osteoarthritis of the talar joints in footballers and ballet dancers. *Acta Orthopaedica Scandinavica* 30:309-314.

de Vries, H. A. 1961. Prevention of muscular distress after exercise. *Research Quarterly* 32(2):77-185.

Dominguez, Richard H, and Gajada, Robert. 1982. *Total body Training.* New York: Warner Books.

Evans, M. 1996. *Instant Stretches for Stress Relief.* New York: Lorenz.

Hubley-Kozey, C. L., and W. D. Standish. 1984. Can stretching prevent athletic injuries? *Journal of Musculoskeletal Medicine* 1(9):25-32.

Iashvili, A.V. 1983. Active and passive flexibility in athletes specializing in different sports. *Soviet Sports Review* 18(1):30-32.

Jacobs, J. 1982. Loosen-up those golf muscles. *Golf World* 21(3):30-31.

Jacobsen, E. *Progressive Relaxation.* 1938. Chicago: University of Chicago Press.

Johns, R. J., and V. Wright. 1962. The relative importance of various tissues in joint stiffness. *Journal of Applied Physiology* 17(5):824-828.

Knott, M., and D. E. Voss. 1968. *Proprioceptive Neuromuscular Facilitation.* New York: Harper and Row.

Lewandowski, P. 1995. To stretch or not to stretch? *Triathlete* 134 (June):106-108, 110.

Mallon, B. 1976. Stretch and strengthen your golf muscles. *Golf Digest* 27(3):98-100.

Moore, M., and R. Hutton. 1980. Electromyographic evaluation of muscle-stretching techniques. *Medicine and Science in Sports and Exercise* 12:322.

Reichley, Melissa. "Roll with It: Swiss Ball Techniques.: Advance for Physical Therapists." September 6, 1993: 10,25.

Richardson, B. 1990. Flexibility. *Australian Golf Digest* (August):84-89.

Vuori, I. 1995. Exercise and physical health: musculoskeletal health and functional capabilities. *Research Quarterly for Exercise and Sport* 66(4):276-285.

Wilson, G. J. 1991. Stretch shortening cycle: Nature and implications for human muscle performance. *Journal of Human Muscle Performance* 1(3):11-31.

CORE EXERCISES 5

The Core Picture

One of your goals as a golf athlete is to maintain both core strength and flexibility. In terms of strength for the core, the need exists to have the core muscle groups balanced and trained in all facets of core movement - flexion or forward bending, extension or rearward bending, lateral flexion or side bending, rotation along the long axis of the spine, and spinal stability. If the core musculature is strong, then your flexibility levels will increase because during the golf swing the individual muscle groups will never be taxed to the point of developing "tightness." Most golf athletes are weak in one of these key facets of spinal strength, and therefore make swing compensations because of the lack of core strength and flexibility abilities.

Remember, flexibility is enhanced when your core training program maintains strength and muscular balance. Your need for formal flexibility training is somewhat based upon the strength and endurance you have in various facets of core movement. However, given the repetitive nature of golf, you will never get to the point that you will need no additional flexibility training. The strengthening and flexibility sections in this program are meant to work in conjunction with each other for their optimal benefit to your golf game.

Like other complex movements, these exercises are more difficult than they first appear. Remember, training on a FitBall® not only requires strength and flexibility, but balance and the use of accessory muscle groups to aid the movement. Refer to Chapter 7 on training equipment to learn how to inflate, care for and otherwise set up the ball and yourself for this program. It is also beneficial to review all the exercises for form and individual adaptation as you progress through the core training programs in the Chapter 6 and demonstrated in the partner video, "FitBall®-Power Golf." When attempting any new exercise, start with the basic version, make sure you have proper form, and use a pace that is slower than you feel you can initially perform.

Warm Up

Pelvic Hip Movement
Forward/Back

Muscle groups: Lower abdominals and erector spinae

Starting position: Seated on the FitBall®, weight evenly distributed, torso in upright position directly over the hips, hand on hips or knees, with knees over feet.

Motion/Finish Position: Move the hips under the shoulders forward and back without moving the shoulders starting first with hip movement without moving the feet, then adding more range of motion of the movement forces you to roll onto your heels and toes with each alternate movement.

Note: This exercise and the subsequent warm up exercises not only prepare the body for core exercise, but they help you to tune into your core and body, raising your kinesthetic or body awareness, a key component of successful golf performance.

Warm Up

Pelvic Hip Movement
Side to Side

Muscle groups: Obliques, quadratus lumborum

Starting position: Seated on the FitBall®, weight evenly distributed, torso in upright position directly over the hips, hand on hips or knees, with knees over feet.

Motion/finish position: Move the hips side to side while keeping the shoulders and head in the same position, gradually adding range of motion so that you are on the sides of your feet.

Warm Up

Pelvic Hip Circles

Muscle groups: Transversus abdominis, rectus abdominus, obliques, quadratus lumborum, psoas and erector spinae

Starting position: Seated on the FitBall®, weight evenly distributed, torso in upright position directly over the hips, hand on hips or knees, with knees over feet.

Motion/finish position: Move the hips first in a clockwise motion adding range of motion while keeping the head and shoulders in the same relative position. After reaching your maximum range of motion, then repeat the same number of circles in a clockwise rotation.

Core Strengthening/Power Exercises

Basic Crunch

Muscle groups: Rectus abdominus, upper portion emphasis

Starting position: Seated on the FitBall®, move to a position where the ball is in the small of the back, just above the hips with the feet directly under the knees, with the hands behind the head or crossed over the chest.

Motion/finish position: While keeping the small of the back on the ball, crunch forward or move your upper chest area and shoulders forward with just the upper portion of the abdominals forward allowing approximately five inches of travel with the shoulders, lower and repeat.

Note: Moving the hands behind the head or raising the hands will add resistance.

Core Strengthening/Power Exercises

Oblique Crunch

Muscle groups: Rectus abdominus, external obliques, internal obliques, and minor contribution from erector spinae.

Starting position: Seated on the FitBall®, move to a position where the ball is in the small of the back, just above the hips with the feet directly under the knees, with one hand behind the head or crossed over the chest and the other hand on the side of the ball for initial support.

Motion/finish position: While keeping the small of the back on the ball, crunch forward and diagonally with just the upper portion of the abdominals with approximately five inches of vertical travel for the shoulders, lower and repeat.

Note: Removing the support hand will force the stabilizer muscles to activate slightly to maintain body and ball position.

Rotating 15's or Progressive Crunches

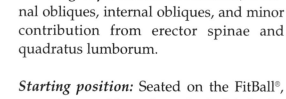

Muscle groups: Rectus abdominus, external obliques, internal obliques, and minor contribution from erector spinae and quadratus lumborum.

Starting position: Seated on the FitBall®, move to a position where the ball is in the small of the back, just above the hips with the feet directly under the knees and one hand behind the head or crossed over the chest, and the other hand on the side of the ball for initial support.

Motion/finish position: While keeping the small of the back on the ball, crunch directly forward/upward first, then return, then crunch again adding 15 degrees to the side, return, then to 30 degrees to the side, return, then to 45 degree angle. You will use the same range of motion vertically for each crunch, just adding progressively more diagonal movement. The correct movement at 45 degrees will feel like you are on one hip pocket.

Note: This exercise is extremely useful for golf because it trains both the external and internal obliques to twist and move at a number of different angles, something which is encountered in various stances in difficult situations such as hills, rough or bunkers.

Core Strengthening/Power Exercises

Side Up

Muscle groups: Obliques, quadratus lumborum and psoas major

Starting position: Start by kneeling next to the ball, then pushing yourself over the top of the ball so the area between your rib cage and hips is on the center of the ball while placing your hands behind your head with your feet staggered for balance.

Motion/finish position: Raise up laterally so your shoulders and head move upward while maintaining trunk contact with the ball being careful to maintain a vertical alignment with your body.

Note: Ball inflation levels and size of FitBall® influence the ease of this exercise, so if you are using two balls, experiment with both to determine which ball is initially easier.

Core Strengthening/Power Exercises

Basic Back Bridge

Muscle groups: Erector spinae, hamstrings(rectus femoris), psoas group, quadratus lumborum

Starting position: From a seated position, slowly roll yourself out on the ball until either the shoulder blades or small of the back rests on the ball while the hips are flexed, with feet almost over the knees, shoulder width apart.

Motion/finish position: Elevate your hips with your knees directly over your feet, so that your back is flat and parallel to the floor.

Note: For beginners, hand position can be over the chest with the ball in the small of the back, while advanced exercisers should place hands in the externally rotated position with the shoulder blades resting on the ball.

Core Strengthening/Power Exercises

Basic Back Bridge with Flexion/Extension and minor stretch

Muscle groups: Erector spinae, hamstrings(rectus femoris), psoas group, quadratus lumborum, hip flexors

Starting position: From a seated position, lower yourself on the ball until either the shoulder blades or small of the back rests on the ball while the hips are flexed, with feet almost over the knees, shoulder width apart.

Motion/finish position: Elevate your hips with your knees directly over your feet, so that your back is flat and parallel to the floor. From that position, move your hips downward or flex at the waist, then come back up to the flat position, and then push yourself over the ball just slightly by extending the hips to a stretch position. Repeat.

Note: This exercise is similar to the squat and arch and builds both core control and kinesthetic sense or body awareness at the same time.

Core Strengthening/Power Exercises

Single Side Alternating Back Bridge

Muscle groups: Erector spinae, hamstrings, psoas group, quadratus lumborum

Starting position: From a seated position, roll yourself out on the ball until either the shoulder blades or small of the back rests on the ball while the hips are flexed, with feet almost over the knees, shoulder width or slightly wider apart.

Motion/finish position: Elevate your hips so you are parallel with the floor, then shift laterally to one side maintaining the basic position, while having the weight on one side of the body, supported on one shoulder blade, with the other side foot resting only on the heel for balance. Hold, then repeat movement to the other side.

Note: For beginners, hand position can be over the chest, while advanced exercisers should place hands in the externally rotated position.

Core Strengthening/Power Exercises

Alternating Single Side Back Bridge with Lateral Flexion

Muscle groups: Erector spinae, hamstrings, psoas group, quadratus lumborum

Starting position: From a seated position, roll yourself out on the ball until either the shoulder blades or small of the back rests on the ball while the hips are flexed, with feet almost over the knees, shoulder width or slightly wider apart.

Motion/finish position: Elevate your hips so you are parallel with the floor, then shift laterally to one side maintaining the basic position, while having the weight on one side of the body, supported on one shoulder blade, with the other side foot resting only on the heel for balance. From this position laterally flex your spine slightly to the un-weighted side while keeping the hips and feet in place. Hold, then repeat movement to the other side.

Core Strengthening/Power Exercises

Single Side Alternating Back Bridge with Flexion/Extension

Muscle groups: Erector spinae, hamstrings, psoas group, quadratus lumborum, hip flexors

Starting position: From a seated position, roll yourself out on the ball until either the shoulder blades or small of the back rests on the ball while the hips are flexed, with feet almost over the knees, shoulder width or slightly wider apart.

Motion/finish position: Elevate your hips so you are parallel with the floor, then shift laterally to one side maintaining the basic position, while having the weight on one side of the body, supported on one shoulder blade, with the other side foot resting only on the heel for balance. Flex your hips/waist down to the floor slightly, then rise back up in reverse fashion going back to parallel with the floor. Hold, then repeat movement to the other side.

Note: Because of the added dimension of flexion and extension, this exercise challenges the stabilizers of the back more than a static or holding bridge, so the golf athlete should take care to maintain a proper bridge position without the unweight leg or hip dipping to the floor.

Core Strengthening/Power Exercises

Single Side Alternating Back Bridge with Flexion/Extension and Spinal Rotation

Muscle groups: Erector spinae, hamstrings, psoas group, quadratus lumborum, transversus abdominis, hip flexors, rectus abdominus

Starting position: From a seated position, roll yourself out on the ball until either the shoulder blades or small of the back rests on the ball while the hips are flexed, with feet almost over the knees, shoulder width or slightly wider apart.

Motion/finish position: Elevate your hips so you are parallel with the floor, then shift laterally to one side maintaining the basic position, while having the weight on one side of the body, supported on one shoulder blade, with the other side foot resting only on the heel for balance. Flex your hips/waist down to the floor slightly, then rise back up in reverse fashion going back to parallel with the floor. Tuck the arm on the un-weighted side into your side or with arms in the "V" position, then roll to that side along the spinal axis with both the shoulders and the hips trying to get the plane of your body vertical to the floor. Hold slightly, then roll back to single side back bridge, then repeat movement to the other side.

Note: This exercise is advanced because of the use of just about every mover and stabilizer in the core system in one exercise.

Core Strengthening/Power Exercises

Rocking Crunch

Muscle groups: Hip flexors, rectus abdominus - lower emphasis

Starting position: From a seated position, place your feet out almost to full extension on your heels with your toes pointed upward.

Motion/finish position: With your hands crossed over chest/behind head or in the externally rotated position, slide your hips and knees forward, bending at the waist rather than the middle back. Raise back up to the seated position bending at the waist/hips being careful not to perform a regular crunch.

Note: This exercise helps to focus on the lower abdominal area where much of the spinal movement in golf occurs.

Core Strengthening/Power Exercises

Rocking Oblique Crunch

Muscle groups: Hip flexors, rectus abdominus - lower emphasis, erector spinae, obliques-both internal and external

Starting position: From a seated position, place your feet out almost to full extension on your heels with your toes pointed upward.

Motion/finish position: With your hands crossed over chest/behind head or in the externally rotated position, slide your hips and knees forward, bending at the waist rather than the middle back. Raise back up diagonally to the seated position bending at the waist/hips being careful not to perform a regular crunch. When in the finish position, your axis point on the ball should be at approximately one of your hip pockets.

Note: This exercise helps to focus on the lower abdominal area where much of the twisting movement in golf occurs.

Core Strengthening/Power Exercises

Rocking Oblique Crunch with Arm/Leg Crossover

Muscle groups: Hip flexors, rectus abdominus - lower emphasis, erector spinae, obliques-both internal and external, psoas group, quadratus lumborum

Starting position: From a seated position, place your feet out almost to full extension on your heels with your toes pointed upward.

Motion/finish position: With your hands crossed over chest/behind head or in the externally rotated position, slide your hips and knees forward, bending at the waist rather than the middle back. Raise back up diagonally to the seated position bending at the waist/hips being careful not to perform a regular crunch and with the opposite leg, flex at the hip and pull towards shoulder. Lower to starting position, then repeat.

Note: This exercise is advanced because of the amount of core control needed to stay on the ball while having only one foot on the floor.

Core Strengthening/Power Exercises

Wood Chop Crunch

Muscle groups: Hip flexors, rectus abdominus - lower emphasis, erector spinae, obliques-both internal and external

Starting position: From a seated position, place your feet out almost to full extension on your heels with your toes pointed upward with both hands at one shoulder or holding a small heavy med ball.

Motion/finish position: With your hands crossed over chest/behind head or in the externally rotated position, slide your hips and knees forward, bending at the waist rather than the middle back. Raise back up diagonally past the seated position bending at the waist/hips being careful to keep your hands or the heavy med ball directly on the shoulder. When in the finish position, your axis point on the ball should be at approximately one of your hip pockets. Finish the set to one side before reversing direction

Note: This is a power version of the rocking oblique crunch because of the increased range of motion and the use of the heavy med ball for advanced exercisers.

Core Strengthening/Power Exercises

Squat to Arch

Muscle groups: Hip flexors, rectus abdominus, erector spinae, psoas group, quadratus lumborum

Starting position: From a seated position, roll your back down on the ball by dropping your hips to the floor and crossing your arms over your chest.

Motion/finish position: Extend with the hips pushing backward over the ball until you are comfortably draped around the contour of the ball with your arms fully extended. Reverse the motion back into the squat position, then repeat attempting to add range of motion on each end of the exercise.

Note: In this dynamic exercise, it is important to make sure your feet are flat on a firm surface for support against the ball in the squat position. In addition, with this being a progressive exercise, it is both a strengthening and stretching exercise at the same time.

Core Strengthening/Power Exercises

Supine Trunk Rotations

Muscle groups: Erector spinae, obliques-both internal and external

Starting position: Start by lying on the floor with your feet flat at 90 degree angle and the ball in your hands directly over your shoulders.

Motion/finish position: While attempting to keep the arms straight, move the ball to one side while moving the knees to the other direction. Hold slightly, reverse direction.

Note: As a progressive exercise, you should add range of motion with each repetition until you reach your maximum with controlled movements in both directions.

Core Strengthening/Power Exercises

Pelvic Hip Lift-Stability or Hold

Muscle groups: Hip flexors, erector spinae, hamstrings

Starting position: Begin by placing the ball between your heels and your calf muscles with shoulders and back on the floor, hands at a 45 degree angle for support.

Motion/finish position: Raise up with the hips until the plane of your entire body is flat, and hold for the prescribed time.
Note: For advanced golf athletes, or when the exercise needs more challenge, move hands to the externally rotated position.

Core Strengthening/Power Exercises

Pelvic Hip Lift-Mobility

Muscle groups: Hip flexors, erector spinae, hamstrings, quadratus lumborum, psoas group

Starting position: Begin by placing the ball between your heels and your calf muscles with shoulders and back on the floor, hands at a 45 degree angle for support.

Motion/finish position: Raise up with the hips until the plane of your entire body is flat, hold briefly, lower to floor and repeat. Note: For advanced golf athletes, or when the exercise needs more challenge, move hands to the externally rotated position.

Core Strengthening/Power Exercises

Pelvic Hip Lift-Lateral Motion

Muscle groups: Hip flexors, erector spinae, hamstrings, quadratus lumborum, psoas group, transversus abdominis

Starting position: Begin by placing the ball between your heels and your calf muscles with shoulders and back on the floor, hands at a 45 degree angle for support.

Motion/finish position: Raise up with the hips until the plane of your entire body is flat, then with the core of the body (not the feet), roll the ball and feet laterally from three to five inches, and then roll the same distance to the other side, repeat.

Note: Most golf athletes will find they have more core control to one side than the other, which is normal in a sport where movements occur predominately to one side. For this reason, you should pay close attention to the amount of lateral travel you possess in both directions, and strive to make the distance equal and to have good form through the entire set.

Core Strengthening/Power Exercises

Single Leg Pelvic Hip Lift

Muscle groups: Hip flexors, erector spinae, hamstrings, quadratus lumborum, psoas group, transversus abdominis

Starting position: Begin by placing the ball between your heels and your calf muscles with shoulders and back on the floor, hands at a 45 degree angle for support.

Motion/finish position: Raise up with the hips until the plane of your entire body is flat, then with the core of the body (not the feet), stabilize yourself against the ball, then supported on one leg, raise the other leg vertically and hold. Lower back to support with both legs, then repeat the sequence with the other leg.

Note: Most golf athletes will find they have more core stability to one side than the other, so you may want to perform an extra set with the weaker side as an advanced exercise.

Core Strengthening/Power Exercises

Seated Single Side Crossovers

Muscle groups: External and internal obliques, erector spinae

Starting position: Seated on the ball with feet flat under knees, place both hands on knees or hips.

Motion/finish position: While maintaining a vertical spine angle and stable hips with one arm, cross over by rotating the spine and shoulders as a unit to one direction. Return to starting position and repeat to the other side adding range of motion with each repetition set.

Note: As a dynamic exercise, this improves the ability to separate the shoulders as a unit from the hips with spinal rotation in the low and mid-back areas.

Core Strengthening/Power Exercises

Spinal Rotation, Seated

Muscle groups: Obliques-external and internal, erector spinae

Starting position: Seated on the ball with feet flat under knees, place both hands together in front of body, parallel to floor.

Motion/finish position: While maintaining a vertical spine angle and stable hips, with both arms, rotate the spine and shoulders as a unit to one direction. Return to starting position and repeat to the other side adding range of motion with each repetition set.

Note: For added resistance, add a heavy med ball held in the hands.

Core Strengthening/Power Exercises

Spinal Rotation, Bridge Position

Muscle groups: Obliques-external and internal, erector spinae, hamstrings, psoas group, quadratus lumborum, transversus abdominis

Starting position: Seated on the ball with feet flat under knees, roll down to the basic back bridge position with the ball either under the shoulder blades or the small of the back, place both hands together in front of body.

Motion/finish position: With both arms, rotate the spine and shoulders as a unit to one direction while maintaining a vertical spine angle and stable hips. Return to starting position and repeat to the other side adding range of motion with each repetition set.

Note: For added resistance, add a heavy med ball held in the hands. This exercise requires the spinal stabilizers to fire and maintain body and ball position, especially when the final arm position is close to parallel to the floor. Initially, until you develop those stabilizers, you may have to re-position yourself on the ball every few repetitions.

Core Strengthening/Power Exercises

Spinal Rotation, 45 degree angle

Muscle groups: Obliques -external and internal, erector spinae, hamstrings, psoas group, quadratus lumborum, transversus abdominis

Starting position: Seated on the ball with feet flat under knees, flex at the hips to drop the hips down towards the floor until you are supported at a 45 degree angle with the ball under the small of the back. Place both hands together in front of body aligned at a 90 degree angle with the spine.

Motion/finish position: With both arms, rotate the spine and shoulders as a unit to one direction while maintaining a vertical spine angle and stable hips. Return to starting position and repeat to the other side adding range of motion with each repetition set.

Note: For added resistance, add a heavy med ball held in the hands. This exercise requires the spinal stabilizers to fire and maintain body and ball position, especially when the final arm position is close to parallel to the floor. Initially, until you develop those stabilizers, you may have to re-position yourself on the ball every few repetitions.

Core Strengthening/Power Exercises

Cat to Prone Back Extension

Muscle groups: Erector spinae

Starting position: With the ball under your abdominal area, hug the ball with your knees and drape your shoulders and chest around the ball.

Motion/finish position: Raise up from the low back, slightly above parallel to the floor with your hands behind your head or in the externally rotated position. Keep your weight on your legs and maintain contact with the ball, hold, repeat.

Note: This exercise always starts with a full cat position to help stretch the low back.

Core Strengthening/Power Exercises

Cat to Airplane

Muscle groups: Erector spinae

Starting position: With the ball under your abdominal area, hug the ball with your knees and drape your shoulders and chest around the ball.

Motion/finish position: Raise up from the low back while straightening the legs so that you are balanced on your abdominal area and with the toes of each foot, hold, repeat.

Note: For advanced golf athletes, move the feet together to challenge the balance system, and while the arms are extended straight, externally rotate the hands for a greater stretch.

Core Strengthening/Power Exercises

Cat to Cobra

Muscle groups: Erector spinae

Starting position: With the ball under your abdominal area, hug the ball with your knees and drape your shoulders and chest around the ball.

Motion/finish position: While pressing with your legs into the ball so that you are balanced on your abdominal area and with the toes of each foot, raise up from the low back. You should attempt to rise as high as comfortably possible with your shoulders externally rotated so that your upper body is as close to vertical as possible.

Note: This is an advanced exercise which requires substantial strength in the core stabilizers as well as better than average flexibility.

Core Strengthening/Power Exercises

Butterfly

Muscle groups: Erector spinae, rectus abdomimus, psoas group, transversus abdominis, quadratus lumborum

Starting position: With the ball under your abdominal area, hug the ball with your knees and drape your shoulders and chest around the ball.

Motion/finish position: Rotate one entire side upwards in one movement pivoting on the opposite side of the ball with the extended arm vertical and the extended leg pointed slightly up in the air. In this position, you should be on one side of the ball with your waist/rib cage area supported on the ball. Hold slightly, lower to cat position, and repeat to other side.

Note: As an advanced stability exercise, this movement fires a number of muscle groups as equal stabilizers and is an effective movement to fight torso sway in the golf swing.

Core Strengthening/Power Exercises

Log Roll

Muscle groups: Erector spinae, obliques, transversus abdominis, psoas group, quadratus lumborum

Starting position: Roll yourself out onto the ball in a "push-up-like" position with the ball either under your knees or your shins with your weight equally balanced between both arms.

Motion/finish position: While maintaining vertical arms, gently roll the ball from side to side under the shins using a rolling motion of the hips rather than a twisting of the feet. Move back to center and repeat to the other side.

Note: As an advanced stability exercise, this adds upper body strength to balance and core control which forces the stabilizers of the core to act to maintain a rod-like body position.

Core Strengthening/Power Exercises

Hip Stand Extension

Muscle groups: Erector spinae, rectus abdominus, transversus abdominis, psoas group, quadratus lumborum

Starting position: Start by hugging the ball in the cat position, then move your hands under you with palms flat against the floor and with elbows tucked into the ball.

Motion/finish position: Move your shoulders towards the floor in a "hand-stand-like" position while maintaining support with the ball and as a unit, extend your legs upward to a position you can comfortably hold, then return to the starting position, repeat.

Note: In this advanced exercise, you have to combine upper body strength with balance, movement and stabilization, and thus you may only be able to hold the position for a few seconds at less than full extension.

Core Flexibility Exercises

Squat to Arch

Muscle groups: Hip flexors, rectus abdominus, erector spinae, psoas group, quadratus lumborum

Starting position: From a seated position, roll your back down on the ball by dropping your hips to the floor and crossing your arms over your chest.

Motion/finish position: Extend with the hips pushing backward over the ball until you are comfortably draped around the contour of the ball with your arms fully extended. Hold, letting gravity stretch you over the contour of the ball. Reverse the motion back into the squat position, then repeat attempting to add range of motion on each end of the exercise and holding the end position slightly longer each time.

Core Flexibility Exercises

Seated Hamstring

Muscle groups: Hamstrings

Starting position: Seated on the ball, both feet flat on the floor.

Motion/finish position: Extend one leg straight on the heel with the toe upward. Slowly push forward from the waist maintaining good posture with the shoulders so the bend comes from the hips. Push to the point of tension, hold at least 10 seconds.

Note: For a more extreme stretch, also roll the hips slightly backward on the ball.

Core Flexibility Exercises

Advanced Trunk Rotation

Muscle groups: Erector Spinae, rectus abdominus, obliques

Starting position: Seated on the ball, both feet flat on the floor in a wider than normal foot position

Motion/finish position: Turning to one side on the ball, keep the forward foot in the same relative position, while moving the back foot as far behind you as possible and still maintaining your balance. With the outside arm to the ball, rotate that arm forward and upwards while you twist along your spinal axis and the arm closest to the ball rotates with the shoulders in the other direction and is pointed outward and down. In this position, the look is similar to the motion of throwing a discus. Hold for at least five seconds, then go back to starting position, then repeat to the other side.

Note: Because this stretch involves the whole body as well as balance and spinal alignment, it is difficult for most golf athletes to perform for more than five seconds at first in good form. Initially, repeat the stretch two or three times to each side until you can work up to 15-20 seconds per side.

Core Flexibility Exercises

Side Stretch

Muscle groups: Obliques and quadratus lumborum

Starting position: Kneeling next to the ball, with the hips directly adjacent to the large part of the ball, place the outside foot a few inches ahead and away from the knee closest to the ball, or start from partially stretched position.

Motion/finish position: Reach over the ball with the hand already resting on the ball, then push with the outside leg so that your waist/rib cage is on top of the ball while you are draped sideways over the ball, and then either return to the starting position, change the ball to the other side, or go directly into the Twisting Side Stretch.

Note: Use gravity to perform the stretch. If you feel out of balance in this position, use the bottom arm to hold onto the ball for additional support.

Core Flexibility Exercises

Twisting Side Stretch

Muscle groups: Obliques, quadratus lumborum

Starting position: Starting in the side stretch position, balanced on the ball, or start next to ball, hugging ball from side position. Then push with the outside leg so that your waist/rib cage is on top of the ball while you are draped sideways over the ball.

Motion/finish position: While holding onto the ball with the bottom hand and arm, reach over the ball with the top arm at approximately a 45 degree angle both diagonally and backwards at the same time. Let your shoulders, torso and hips spin so that you are almost lying horizontally on the ball. Make sure to reach with the extended hand to facilitate additional stretch in the shoulder and chest area.

Note: While gravity helps with this stretch, its full effectiveness is when you actively reach with the extended arm.

Core Flexibility Exercises

Bent Knee Ball Roll

Muscle groups: Erector spinae, obliques, hip area

Starting position: Lying on the floor, with arms outstretched, place the ball against the back of your thighs using a slight curl motion of the knee to hold onto the ball.

Motion/finish position: Keeping your arms flat on the floor, slowly twist the ball to one side using your knees until you feel tension, pause briefly and repeat the motion to the other side adding range of motion to each repetition set.

Note: As a dynamic stretch, this can be done on an alternating tempo. As a static or hold stretch, you can go all the way to one side and hold for five or more seconds before going to the other side.

Core Flexibility Exercises

Kneel and Bow

Muscle groups: Quadratus lumborum, obliques

Starting position: In a kneeling position with hips over the knees, back parallel to the floor. Arms are fully extended onto the ball with the head tucked between the arms looking at the floor.

Motion/finish position: Alternating hands, slowly work or roll the ball to one side while maintaining the direction of your hips and legs by bending laterally along the length of the spine. Use your hands on the ball for support and to accentuate the stretch. Hold for at least 10 seconds, then repeat to the other side.

Note: During the golf season this is an ideal stretch to counter-act the effects of swinging and crunching primarily on one side.

References

Chappuis, J.L. and G.D. Johnson. 1995. The "super six" stretches for golfers. *The Physician and Sportsmedicine* 23(4):87-88.

Dominguez, Richard H, and Gajada, Robert. 1982. *Total body Training*. New York: Warner Books.

Egoscue, P. 1992. *The Egoscue Method of Health Through Motion*. New York: Harper Collins Publishers.

Larkin, A.F., W.F. Larkin, W.F. Larkin II, and S.L. Larkin. 1990. Annual torso-specific conditioning program for golfers. In A.J. Cochran, ed., *Science and Golf: Proceedings of the First World Scientific Congress of Golf*. London: EF&N, Spon.

Kravitz, L., and D. Kosich. 1993. Flexibility: a comprehensive research review and program design guide. *IDEA Today* 11(6):42-49.

Ross, M.D. 1995. Stretching the hamstrings. *Strength and Conditioning* 17(6):35-36.

Vermeil, A., and L. Dennis. 1985. Get stronger, get better. Four easy-to-do exercises that will increase your power and control on the course. *Golf Digest* 36(4):57-60.

Wolkodoff, N. 1987. Resistance training for endurance athletes. *American Ski Coach* 10(5):31.

——. 1990. In-season plyometrics: Maintaining and developing functional strength. *American Ski Coach* 13(5):10-11.

——. 1995. *Flexibility Exercises For Better Golf*. Denver, CO: ExerTrends.

CORE ROUTINES 6

Stability, Rotation, Then Power

As you pursue better golf through this program, it is important to note that the following routines first build spinal stability in the swing. This is the foundation of the golf stance. Without spinal stability and control, rotation and rotational power will not be effective and will be inconsistent.

Flexibility will be at its optimal levels through developing core strength and muscular balance. The flexibility programs and strength programs are meant to work together. This combination will decrease your need for formal flexibility training to a certain degree. However, given the repetitive nature of golf, you will never get to the point that you will need no additional flexibility training. The strengthening and flexibility sections in this program are meant to work in conjunction with each other to produce optimal benefit to your golf game.

Like any other complex movement, these exercises are more difficult than they first appear. Remember, training on a FitBall® not only requires strength and flexibility, but balance and the use of accessory muscle groups to aid the movement. Refer to Chapter 7 regarding training equipment on how to inflate, care for and otherwise set up the ball and yourself for this program.

It is beneficial to review all the exercises for form and individual adaptation as you progress through the core training programs in the routines sections and demonstrated in the partner video, "FitBall®-Power Golf." When attempting any new exercise, start with the basic version, make sure you have proper form, and use a pace that is slower than you feel you can initially perform.

The routines are designed to build the necessary golf characteristics sequentially in each series:

Golf Stance. These three routines stress the ability to maintain basic position at address and core angle and stability during movement

Rotational Energy. These two routines combine core stability from various angles with the ability to turn the shoulders and upper back independent of the hips and low back.

Rotational Power. The most challenging movement-based routines in this program, these two programs combine stability, rotation and the ability to generate power through both movement and the maintenance of proper position.

Counter-Balance. Because the golf swing involves repetitive movements in basically one direction, it is important during the golf season to perform some core training to put the body back into balance, in order to restore flexibility and function. These routines place the body back into muscular core balance with both static and dynamic exercises and should be performed two to three times per week in the golf season as need arises.

Flexibility. Because flexibility and strength are related, you should perform this short stretching routine after each exercise session or golf session.

Routine Progressions

Progressing through the routines in the designated order will have the best effect on your golf game because the subsequent abilities needed in each routine are built upon the training in the previous routine. Because of this fact, you should perform each routine at least three times, and preferably four or five times before moving on to the next routine. The progression which will move you from building basic strength to rotational power should take somewhere between 30-45 days. If you rush the process, you will not build the basic abilities that each routine is designed to do, and your body will not gain the full effects from the next routine or may not have the ability to perform those exercises and sequences correctly.

Depending upon the amount of golf you are playing while using these routines, you may have to perform the routines every other day with the flexibility program every day after golf. If you can't perform the exercises in good form and with a proper tempo through the whole routine, then it's time for modification which could be as simple as fewer repetitions, or just taking a day off from the program. Listen to your body as you should with any exercise program.

On days when you feel tired or not as core strong, you can drop back to the previous routine, or lessen the number of repetitions, or decrease the difficulty level. Ways to make the basic routine more challenging are included at the end of each workout routine. The goal repetitions are what you should be able to perform the first or second time through the routine. Initially, each routine will take slightly longer than the average of 4+ minutes because of getting used to changing positions on the ball and exercise familiarity.

As you progress through each program, try to add more repetitions, difficulty via positioning, extra resistance with the heavy med balls or additional stability/balance challenge with the disco sits. The suggested means for adding difficulty and challenge is listed at the end of each routine with a suggested order of progression.

WARM UP

Pelvic Hip Movements, Forward - Back

goal: 10 repetitions

Pelvic Hip Movements, Side to Side

goal: 10 repetitions to each side (Right/Left)

Pelvic Circles

goal: 5 repetitions each direction

Adding Difficulty/Challenge:

- Add more range of motion to each exercise.
- Place a disco sit balance cushion under one foot for balance challenge.
- Add Squat to Arch to the warm up routine.

GOLF STANCE 1

Basic Crunch

goal: 10+ repetitions

Back Bridge

goal: 20+ seconds

Oblique Crunch

goal: 10 repetitions to each side

Rocking Crunch

goal: 10+ repetitions

Squat to Arch

goal: 5+ repetitions

Pelvic Hip Lift Stability

goal: 20+ seconds

Adding difficulty/challenge:

- Add 10 more repetitions for the Basic Crunch and the Squat to Arch.
- Add 20 seconds for the Pelvic Hip Lift-Stability.
- You should perform this entire routine for 5 days before proceeding to Golf Stance 2.

GOLF STANCE 2

Back Bridge

goal: 20+ seconds

Oblique Crunch

goal: 10+ repetitions to each side

Alternating Single Side Bridge

goal: 5 movements to each side

Rocking Crunch

goal: 10 repetitions

Side Up

goal: 10 repetitions to each side

Cat to Back Extension

goal: 10 repetitions

Adding difficulty/challenge:

- Add 10 more repetitions for the rocking crunch and Cat to Back Extension.

- Add 20 seconds for the Back Bridge.

- If you can master this routine within one session, then you can add one disco sit under a foot during the static or holding exercises to further challenge your balance.

- You should perform this entire routine for 5 days before proceeding to Golf Stance 3.

GOLF STANCE 3

Oblique Crunch

goal: 10 repetitions to each side

Rocking Crunch

goal: 10 repetitions

Spinal Rotation in Bridge Position

goal: 10 repetitions to each side

Alternating Single Side Bridge

goal: 5 repetitions to each side

Cat to Airplane

goal: 10 repetitions

Pelvic Hip Lift Mobility

goal: 10 repetitions

Adding Difficulty/Challenge:

- Add 5 repetitions to each side in the Alternating Single Side Bridge, then hold each movement R/L for 3 seconds before shifting back to the other side.

- Add 20 repetitions to the Pelvic Hip Lift-Mobility, then move hands to externally rotated position for greater core instability and training effect.

- You should perform this entire routine for 5 days before proceeding to Rotational Energy 1.

ROTATIONAL ENERGY 1

Seated Single Side Crossovers

goal: 5 repetitions each side

Alternating Single Side Bridge with Flexion/Extension and Spinal Rotation

goal: 5 repetitions each side

Spinal Rotation Bridge Position

goal: 10 repetitions each side

Rocking Oblique Crunch

goal: 5 repetitions each side

Pelvic Hip Lift-Lateral Motion

goal: 5 repetitions each side

Supine Trunk Rotation

goal: 5 repetitions each side

Adding Difficulty/Challenge:

- Add 10 repetitions to each side in the Supine Trunk Rotation.
- Add the use of a heavy med ball for the Spinal Rotation Bridge Position, then add 10 additional repetitions to each side.
- Add 10 repetitions to each side for the Pelvic Hip Lift-Lateral motion.
- Add 5 repetitions to each side for the Rocking Oblique Crunch.
- Add Log Roll, 5 repetitions each side.
- Perform this routine for 4 sessions before moving to Rotational Energy 2.

ROTATIONAL ENERGY 2

Spinal Rotations Seated

goal: 5 repetitions each side

Alternating Single Side Bridge with Flexion/Extension and Spinal Rotation

goal: 5 repetitions each side

Rotating 15's

goal: 2 sets to each side

Pelvic Hip Lift-Lateral Motion

goal: 10 repetitions each side

Wood Chop Crunch

goal: 10 repetitions each side

Pelvic Hip Lift-One Leg

goal: 20 seconds each side

Adding Difficulty/Challenge:

- Add 2 additional sets to Rotating 15's.
- Use heavy med ball on spinal rotations, then increase to 15 repetitions.
- Increase time on Pelvic Hip Lift-One Leg to 30 seconds.
- Perform this routine at least 3 sessions before moving to Rotational Power 1.

ROTATIONAL POWER 1

Rocking Crunch

goal: 10 repetitions

Alternating Single Side Bridge with Flexion/Extension and Spinal Rotation

goal: 5 repetitions each side

Spinal Rotation 45 Degrees

goal: 10 repetitions each side

Butterfly

goal: 5 repetitions each side

Wood Chop Crunch

goal: 10 repetitions each side

Cat to Airplane

goal: 10 repetitions

Adding Difficulty/Challenge:

- Add 20 repetitions to the Rocking Crunch.
- Add 10 repetitions to the Wood Chop Crunch.
- Add 5 repetitions to Butterfly.
- Add Log Roll, 10 repetitions each side.
- Hold each Cat to Airplane for 5 seconds.
- Perform this routine for at least 3 sessions before moving to Rotational Power 2.

ROTATIONAL POWER 2

Cat to Airplane

goal: 5 repetitions

Alternating Single Side Bridge with Flexion/Extension and Spinal Rotation

goal: 10 repetitions each side

Pelvic Hip Lift - Lateral Motion

goal: 10 repetitions each side

Rocking Oblique Crunch

goal: 10 repetitions each side

Spinal Rotation in Bridge Position

goal: 10 repetitions each side

Squat to Arch

goal: 5 repetitions

Adding Difficulty/Challenge:
- Add 5 repetitions to Pelvic Hip Lift - Lateral Motion.
- Add Hip Stand Extension 2 x 10 seconds.
- Add 10 repetitions to Rocking Oblique Crunch
- Add heavy med ball to Spinal Rotation in Bridge Position.

COUNTER BALANCE 1

Alternating Single Side Bridge with Lateral Flexion

goal: 5 repetitions each side

Cat to Cobra

goal: 5 repetitions

Basic Crunch

goal: 15 repetitions

Oblique Crunch

goal: 15 repetitions L to R, 5 repetitions R to L (If left handed, reverse this sequence)

Side Up

goal: 5 repetitions on Left or Target Side, 15 repetitions on Right or Non-Target Side

Squat to Arch

goal: 10 repetitions

Adding Difficulty/Challenge:

- Add 5 repetitions to Cat to Cobra.
- Add 15 repetitions to Basic Crunch.
- Add 10 repetitions to Squat to Arch.

COUNTER BALANCE 2

Back Bridge with Flexion/Extension and Minor Stretch

goal: 10 repetitions

Supine Trunk Rotations

goal: 20 repetitions to each side

Pelvic Hip Lift -One Leg

goal: 15 seconds on R leg, 15 seconds on L leg, 15 seconds on R leg

Rocking Oblique Crunch

goal: 10 repetitions L to R, 10 repetitions R to L, 10 repetitions L to R

Alternating Single Side Bridge

goal: 15 repetitions Middle to R, 5 repetitions Middle to L, 15 repetitions Middle to R

Bent Knee Ball Roll

goal: 15 repetitions to each side

Adding Difficulty/Challenge:

- Add 10 repetitions to Rocking Oblique Crunch, each direction.
- Add 10 seconds to Pelvic Hip Lift-One Leg.
- Add 10 repetitions to Back Bridge with Flexion/Extension and Minor Stretch.
- Add Hip Stand Extension, 15 seconds.

115

FLEXIBILTY DEVELOPMENT

Squat to Arch

goal: 5 repetitions holding stretch for at least 3 seconds

Advanced Trunk Rotation

goal: Hold for 10 seconds each side

Seated Hamstring

goal: Hold for 15 seconds each side

Side Stretch

goal: Hold for 10 seconds each side

Twisting Side Stretch

goal: Hold for 10 seconds each side

Kneel and Bow

goal: Hold for 15 seconds each side

Adding Difficulty/Challenge:

- Add Supine Trunk Rotation, 20 repetitions after Squat to Arch.
- Hold Side Stretch for 20 seconds each side.
- Add Supine Trunk Rotations, 15 repetations to each side, as first exercise.
- Add Bent Knee Ball Roll, 10 repetitions to each side.

References

Allerheilegen, B., and R. Rogers. 1995. Plyometrics program design. *Strength and Conditioning* 17(4):26-31.

Beaulieu, R.A. 1981. Developing a stretching program. *The Physician and Sportsmedicine* 9(11):59-69.

Bloomfield, J. 1979. Modifying human physical capacities and technique to improve performance. *Sports Coach* 3:19-25.

Bompa, T.O. 1983. *Theory and Methodology of Training.* Dubuque, IA: Kendall/Hunt.

————. 1993. Periodization of Strength: *The New Wave in Resistance Training.* Toronto: Veritas Publishing.

Fleck, S., and W. Kraemer. 1996. *Periodization Breakthrough!* Ronkonkoma, NY: Advanced Research Press, Inc.

Gilliam. G.M. 1981. Effects of frequency of weight training on muscle strength enhancement. *Journal of Sports Medicine* 21:432-436.

Hahn, A.G. 1992. Physiology of training. In J. Bloomfield, P.A. Fricker, and K.D. Fitch, eds., *Textbook of Science and Medicine in Sport. Victoria,* Australia: Blackwell Scientific Publications.

Hakkinen, K. 1985. Factors influencing trainability of muscular strength during short term and prolonged training. *National Strength and Conditioning Association Journal* 7:32-37.

Koutedakis, Y. 1995. Seasonal variation in fitness parameters in competitive athletes. *Sports Medicine* 19(6):373-392.

Kraemer, W.J. 1983. Exercise prescription in weight training: A needs analysis. *National Strength and Conditioning Association Journal* 5:64-65.

Kurtz, T. 1991. *Science of Sports Training.* Island Pond, VT: Stadion Press.

Larkin, A.F., W.F. Larkin, W.F. Larkin II, and S.L. Larkin. 1990. Annual torso-specific conditioning program for golfers. In A.J. Cochran, ed., Science and Golf: *Proceedings of the First World Scientific Congress of Golf.* London: E. & F.N Spon.

Poliquin, C., and P. Patterson. 1989. Classification of strength qualities. *National Strength and Conditioning Association Journal* 11(6):48-50.

Ross, M.D. 1995. Stretching the hamstrings. *Strength and Conditioning* 17(6):35-36.

Roundtable. 1984. Flexibility, *National Strength and Conditioning Association Journal* 10:73.

Sleamaker, R. 1989. *Serious Training for Serious Athletes.* Champaign, IL: Human Kinetics.

Selye, H. 1956. *The Stress of Life.* New York: McGraw-Hill.

Spassov, A. 1988. Constructing training programs: Part II. *National Strength and Conditioning Association Journal* 10(5):65-70.

Stone, M.H. et al. 1982. A theoretical model of resistance training. *National Strength and Conditioning Association Journal* 3(5):36-39.

Syster, B., and G. Stull. 1970. Muscular endurance retention as a function of length of detraining. *Research Quarterly Exercise and Sport* 41:105.

Wathen, D. 1987. Flexibility: Its place in warm-up activities. *NSCA Journal* 9(5):26-27.

Wilson, G.J. 1996. Weight training program design: Importance of muscular recovery and prevention of over-training. *Network* 8(6)30-32.

Wolkodoff, N. 1987. Resistance training for endurance athletes. *American Ski Coach* 10(5):31.

———. 1990. In-season plyometrics: Maintaining and developing functional strength. *American Ski Coach* 13(5):10-11.

TRAINING EQUIPMENT

Ball Size

Make sure you have a properly sized and inflated FitBall® before beginning this program. For most golf athletes, a 65 c.m. ball is suitable for average sized individuals for the exercises in this program. To check the size of your ball for your use, sit on the ball in an erect posture with your knees directly over your feet. If this angle is 90 degrees or greater, then the ball is of proper size.

For added exercise effectiveness, it is desirable to acquire a FitBall® which is slightly larger than the one you use normally for training, such as a 75 c.m. FitBall®. The larger size and pressure difference will force the spinal stabilizers to work differently, enhancing the training effect. In the passive stretches, where gravity is pulling you over the ball, the different size ball will develop flexibility in different areas and further challenge your balance system.

Ball Inflation and Care

Before inflating the ball, you need an idea of the maximum size which is printed on the FitBall® under the logo. A 65 c.m. ball should be inflated to a maximum of 25 inches in diameter, and a 75 c.m. ball inflated to a maximum diameter of 29 inches. Using a yard stick or measuring tape, mark the appropriate spot on a wall or door, and when inflating the ball, make sure not to exceed the maximum recommended diameter.

When inflating the FitBall®, gently remove the air plug, and place the portable pump nozzle or a low-power pump, such as an air mattress compress nozzle, into the filler tube. Inflate the ball to the recommended height, and then firmly insert the air plug.

When using the ball, remove any sharp objects such as

keys, pens, jewelry or similar items in your pockets or attached to your clothing which may cause the ball to be punctured. Similarly, only use the ball indoors as outside exercise can gouge or tear the ball's surface. If the ball has a deep gouge or scratch, replace the ball. Your FitBall® should also be cleaned periodically with a soft cloth and a mild detergent, rinsed and then dried. Never use abrasive or strong cleaners, as they may mar the ball's surface. Finally, keep the ball away from heat sources and out of direct sunlight.

Ball Safety

Like any vigorous exercise program, consult your physician or health care professional before beginning this program. Always begin slowly, and strive to perform each exercise in a controlled manner with attention to form. Only advance to more difficult versions of each routine when you have fully mastered each routine and each specific exercise fully.

Space is important for the exercise routines, so make sure the area is free of furniture or other hard objects and the surface is carpeted to provide good traction. Initially, perform the exercises with good athletic footwear, as this will give you more support and contact with the floor. When using the FitBall®, clothing should be loose and comfortable and allow for a full range of motion while maintaining contact with the ball.

Balance Enhancement

For an additional training benefit for dynamic balance and increased kinesthetic awareness, add one or two disco sit cushions to place under your feet during the exercises. This will provide a de-stabilizing effect, and further challenge your core muscles and balance system. These cushions should be inflated to different levels to provide varying degrees of instability. For advanced golf exercises focusing on an additional core challenge, these cushions can also be placed under the feet during upper-body resistance exercises on the ball. Remember, only use the cushions and other balance-challenging devices once you have mastered the basic and advanced exercises with good form.

Additional Resistance

Adding resistance to exercises is as simple as holding a heavy med ball during selected exercises such as spinal rotations and the wood chop crunch. These balls come in a variety of weights, and generally two balls weighing 1000 grams and 2000 grams are adequate for most people to add extra resistance for core exercises such as the wood chop crunch or spinal rotations in the bridge position.

References

Cardinal, B.J. 1994. Six steps to selecting exercise equipment. *Athletic Business* 18(9):39-40,42,45,47.

Kato, D. 1992. A buyer's guide to exercise equipment. *Guide pour l'achat d'appareils d'exercices.* CAHPER journal /Journal de l'ACSEPL 58(2)38-39.

Ramotar, J. 1993. Injuries from exercise equipment. *The Physician and Sportsmedicine* 21(2):59.

Shafran, J. 1995. Stay in, work out: home-exercise equipment that you'll want to spend some quality time with. *Women's Sports & Fitness* 17(8):57-60.

Stamford, B. 1997. Choosing and using exercise equipment. *The Physician and Sportsmedicine* 25(1):107-108.

Wolkodoff, N. 1993. Exercising equipment options for the home. *Rocky Mountain News: Special Health & Fitness Issue* 3-5.

Wolkodoff, N. and A.M. Miller. 1995. Recommending home equipment: part 2 — strength training. *Certified News* 5(1):9-10.

GLOSSARY

Active Flexibility. The use of opposing muscle groups by the individual to move the joint or set of joints through a motion.

Aerobic Capacity. The actual amount of oxygen that can combine with fat and carbohydrates in the muscle cell to produce steady or constant muscular work, which is influenced by training variables.

Ballistic Stretch. Any stretch or movement with enough force or speed to activate the stretch reflex resulting in a rapid movement the other direction.

Cardiovascular Fitness. The general ability of the body to perform long-term exercise or activities lasting 20 minutes or more without fatigue.

Concentric contraction. Muscular work where the muscle shortens, generally raising a weight or lifting body weight away from gravity.

Delayed Onset of Muscular Soreness (DOSM). The after-effect of heavy muscular work, either severe energy system or resistance training, which causes the muscle to have physical trauma, including internal swelling, generally becoming greatest 24 to 48 hours after the exercise session.

Dynamic Flexibility. The use of any method that involves movement to increase range of motion around a joint or set of joints.

Eccentric Contraction. A muscular contraction where the muscle actually lengthens, generally against an external resistance such as a weight or gravity.

Elastic Energy. The amount of stored energy present when a muscle, ligament, tendon or group of same are stretched.

Energy System Training. Any major body movement training, such as cycling, stair climbing or jogging, where intensity or difficulty can vary from aerobic to anaerobic levels.

Exercise Duration. The actual length of any exercise bout or session measured in minutes.

Exercise Frequency. The number of specific exercise sessions of any type or total during the period of one week.

Exercise Intensity. The effort of the exercise, which in energy system training is generally a percentage of aerobic capacity or maximum heart rate, and in the case of resistance training is the number of repetitions performed within a given time frame with a specific resistance.

Fast Oxidative Glycolytic Muscle Fibers. Referred to as FOG fibers, those muscle fibers or units of movement that have almost equal aerobic and power characteristics and are trainable in either direction.

Fast Twitch Muscle Fibers. Those muscle fibers or units of movement commonly labeled FT, that are strength and power oriented with relatively low muscular endurance.

Flexibility. The demonstrated ability to move specifically through a range of motion either statically or dynamically.

Functional Strength. The ability to move in a controlled manner in a situation or movement which has muscular and coordination demands similar to the target activity.

Isometric Contraction. Muscular movement that is almost stationary against a resistance.

Kcal. The kilocalorie, or the amount of energy required to raise one kilogram of water one degree Celsius; the measure of food energy and human work, expressed as kcals.

Muscular Endurance. The general or specific ability to repeat a movement without fatigue or a decrease in coordination or performance.

Muscular Failure. A level of work where the muscle cannot continue because of lack of fuel, lack of recovery or neurological failure, known as MF.

Passive Flexibility. The level of flexibility where an external force, such as an exercise partner or trainer, pushes a joint or set of joints through their range of motion.

Plyometric Training. Training where a rapid eccentric movement is followed immediately by a quick and powerful concentric movement, such as catching and then throwing a medicine ball.

Power. The ability to move as rapidly as possible against a resistance or through a movement.

Proprioceptive Neuromuscular Facilitation. Known as PNF, a set of varied stretching techniques that use combinations of contractions, relaxation and movement of muscles and joints in question.

Range of Motion. Termed ROM, the collective movement through a joint or set of joints, which is influenced by muscle, ligament, tendon and skin resistance.

Set. A group of repetitions performed consecutively or nearly consecutively.

Slow Twitch Muscle Fibers. Those muscle fibers or units of movement that are endurance-oriented with relatively low muscular power levels, known as ST units.

Static Flexibility. The ability to move through ROM and hold a position.

Strength. Defined as force against or through a resistance regardless of how much time the effort takes.

Stretch Reflex. The reaction of the muscle spindles, or protective mechanisms inside the muscle, when stretched too far, sending a signal to the brain and back to the muscle to contract, protecting the body from injury and aiding movement.

Training Load. The quantifiable amount of training stress put on the system or muscle in any given exercise that can be measured in kcal per hour, speed, grade, resistance or V02 for energy system training, and actual resistance used in resistance training.

INDEX

RESOURCE LIST

The following products or services are listed on this page as a service for readers who seek further information. This information is provided as a service only and does not constitute an endorsement by KickPoint Press.

Ball Dynamics/FitBall®   www.balldynamics.com
(800) 752-2255
      FitBall® Stability and Training balls
      Heavy Med Plyometric balls
      Disco Sit Balance Cushions
      FitBall® Core Powered Golf Video

Bite Golf Shoes   www.biteshoes.com
(800) 248-3465

Dimension Z Golf Clubs   www.dimensionz.com
(888) 271-1889

Neil Wolkodoff/Physical Golf
www.physicalgolf.com
A wide variety of training services are available including comprehensive one day and two-day programs, group presentations, on-going training via email and fax, and golf-fitness center design.

To order additional copies of Core Powered Golf...

If you borrowed this book from a friend or library, and wish to purchase your own copy, and do not have distribution through your local bookstore, Core Powered Golf can be ordered direct by calling (800) 966-4767 toll-free. Inquiries on special market orders, premiums, trade markets, and gift sales should be directed to KickPoint Press at (303) 571-9335.

NOTES

NOTES